Squash – Beyond the Basics

Squash- Beyond the Basics

Ian Robinson and David Bond

 Springfield Books Limited

©1986 Ian Robinson and David Bond

Published by Springfield Books Limited, Norman Road, Denby Dale,
Huddersfield HD8 8TH, West Yorkshire, England.

First edition 1986

ISBN 0 947655 16 6 (cased)
ISBN 0 947655 17 4 (paperback)

British Library CIP data
Robinson, Ian, 1952–
Squash – beyond the basics.
1. Squash rackets (Game)
I. Title   II. Bond, David
796.34'3   GV1004

Design: Douglas Martin Associates
Line drawings by John Dillow
Photography: All photographs are by Stephen Line except the following:
    pages 30, 62, 64 Tim Pike (Sporting Prints);
    pages 42, 45, 48, 51 Graham Mathers;
    page 136 Steve Powell (All-Sport).
Frontispiece: Ian Robinson
Cover picture: Qamar Zaman (photo: All-Sport)
Typesetting and origination: Armitage Typo/Graphics Ltd, Huddersfield
Printed and bound in England by The Bath Press

Contents

1. An introduction to squash

The attraction of squash must surely be traced at its simplest to the fascination of striking a ball against a wall with a kind of bat with sufficient control to ensure that the ball returns to the sender. It would be interesting to know how many eminent world stars in other sports began their careers by striking a ball to a wall in just such a fashion. Man's desire to compete is readily served in squash terms by adding three more walls, certain rules, and an opponent to test a player's prowess.

Rumour has it that a prison cell was the original squash court, but suffice it to say that the upper classes were the first to latch on to the idea. The public schools, the universities and the services all served as breeding-grounds for the young sport, which thus reached some far-flung corners of what was then the British Empire, most notably Pakistan. The sport quickly expanded further; this is highlighted by the way in which Hashim Khan, who was to become the British Open champion on seven occasions, was introduced to it. In Pakistan the squash courts do not have roofs, and the young Hashim was readily available as a ball boy to return the ball to the court whenever the British officers hit it outside. But in between Hashim would sneak on to the courts and, using any racket he could lay hands on, practise the skills which were eventually going to turn him into a squash legend. This was the beginning of the breakdown of the hold the upper classes had on the sport, for other players at once followed his lead. In a similar way Jonah Barrington, a Cornishman by birth and an Irishman by adoption, was to popularise the sport in Britain. Barrington won six British Open titles of his own, but also brought a missionary zeal to the sport, promoting and nurturing its broader interests for a wider public.

The authors of this book offer their ideas and views about squash from a background of more than twelve years' tournament playing and work in squash clubs, to the three million or more who play the sport for fun and recreation or for a living. A major objective is for the reader to see the overriding point of playing the sport – that of enjoyment – but at the same time to

approach it with the idea that there is always something to learn and always a way to improve personal standards.

Despite what some players say, there is nobody who really enjoys losing. But there may be a different way of approaching the sport that will give the player – at both club level or higher – a more accessible means of improving his standards. Squash at a superficial level has long projected the image solely of fitness. The virtues of patience, attrition and long-lasting rallies down the backhand-side wall have dominated much of the thinking and convinced the majority that it is a game of sheer physical survival in which it is nearly impossible to strike the ball anywhere in the court that will be out of an opponent's reach. This may or may not be the case to a degree, but it is far from being the whole story; here it is intended to examine the sport in a way which aims to broaden the view of the majority and to offer some players an informed basis for deeper insight.

Squash is not just a question of fitness and attiriton, otherwise the shapes and sizes of the players who dominate the sport at the highest level would not be as different as they palpably are. There are players like the former British champion Gawain Briars, who stands nearly 6ft 5in, or New Zealander Stuart Davenport, who is of similar build except that he is slightly thinner, standing alongside Pakistan's Gogi Alauddin, the former world amateur champion, who is small and thin by comparison. In contrast to Alauddin is his fellow countryman, Hiddy Jahan, a runner-up in the British Open, far sturdier and near 6ft in height. All these players have been – and in some cases still are – ranked among the top ten players in the world. Jonah Barrington, arguably the most famous name in the world of squash, is a small man, but as a result of his fanatical devotion he attended to every detail of fitness and thus created a new interest in a hitherto neglected concept. Barrington promoted this major aspect of the sport, quite possibly without realising what an effect this concept might have on its development. But it should be made quite clear that while he honed his level of fitness, he was also paying attention to his racket skills with the same zeal, even though his work on the latter did not generate anything like the same amount of interest as his attention to the former.

The game itself is the most important matter, and attention will here be focused mainly on aspects of its skills. The physical requirements will also be assessed at the appropriate time, but hopefully they will be viewed in balance with a total consideration of the sport.

The most successful squash player ever produced in the UK – Jonah Barrington

Squash will have lost many enthusiasts and loyal players in recent years because of their overriding belief that there is really no point in participating because they are not of the required physical proportions or standards and are not in a position to work for these. But the current trend is towards health and fitness, and this may in turn mean that those who always believed that they were not of a suitable physical type might be attracted back to the sport. Learning to play squash for its own sake is possible for people of all shapes and sizes, provided that sensible health precautions are taken at the start and at regular intervals thereafter – but this is no more than the average person would need to consider in normal working life.

Squash itself has a delightful way of allowing each player the chance to express his personality through the style in which he chooses to play. Choice of stroke, power, touch, subtlety, surprise, height, width and accuracy all go towards creating a fascinating backcloth against which to paint the picture of squash, with all the spaces on the court being used and the players' rackets dictating to the ball. The sport has already thrown up some most unusual players, who have added to the basic dimensions of the game through their personal style, but it is still perhaps in the early days of its overall development. The exciting possibility exists that the sport has only scratched the surface in realising its full potential of artistic and tactical as well as technical advancement.

Qamar Zaman of Pakistan, the 1974 world champion, is an example of one of the most recent innovators in the sport; Zaman insisted on attacking the front corners at a time when players were by and large training hard for fitness and attacking the back corners. Zaman has a lethal range of racket skills and ball control; equally, he is a master of disguise and deception. These qualities are all allied to a fine deadpan sense of humour; and together make him an interesting exponent of the sport. In addition, Zaman is able to attack the front of the court with such accuracy and lowness over the tin that his opponent has to be remarkably swift to return the ball and rapidly assumes the role of a demented dog merely fetching and carrying at his master's beck and call. In 1974 Zaman succeeded in beating all the world's best players, culminating in victory in the British Open, which was acknowledged at the time to be the world championships and was certainly squash's equivalent to Wimbledon.

In the world's major events so far, the strokemaker has not

Qamar Zaman – a player of immense racket skills and innovative shot making

had an overall domination of the winner's rostrum because the more prudent disciplinarians have used the strokes with more care and less ambition in an attempt to create a more frequent winning formula. But this does not alter the fact that such champions have had a full range of strokes at their disposal and have been capable of using them, even if they have restricted the usage in order to produce that winning formula.

The example of Qamar Zaman is a good one to encourage the beginner to learn to express his individualistic talents, but there are some basic principles that need to be absorbed first. The starting-point will always be at a very basic level, for which there can be no apology, because it provides an opportunity to define terms and to ensure that the beginner has a proper foundation on which to base his search for his own favourite strokes and rally-winning tactics. Such a foundation is always essential because there will inevitably be periods of loss of form and tactical complication, which can be corrected most readily by using only the basic essentials of driving the ball safely to the back corners.

It is always valid to start from the basic premise that if the player hits the ball to the front wall on one more occasion than his opponent, then the rally will be won. This may be stating the obvious and be a marvellous simplification, but it should always be in the forefront of the player's mind, particularly if the match is not progressing according to the desired plan. The most important factor is that the player should not be satisfied to make that plan the *only* tactical option, because that will handicap his improvement when there is more to be learnt in the game. It will also leave the player vulnerable to an opponent who has spotted his tactical ploy and tries to make life difficult for him if he sticks to the same plan; its predictability delivers the initiative to the opponent. Flexibility is the player's main asset; he must be able to select other ways of conducting rallies against a wily opponent. To be flexible, however, the player must have equal facility in all areas of match play; so if the discussion of technique in the early stages seems obvious, that may be because it is a question of revamping the player's original thinking in order that the strokes and stroke production can ultimately be advanced to create opportunities of opening up further attacking ploys in the rally.

It is hoped that in rethinking the basics, the player will come to see aspects that may have been overlooked, or ways of creating new options. The player should always be on the lookout for different methods of winning rallies and should use practice sessions to experiment, first including and finally perfecting new strokes. If the player adopts this philosophy, it is certainly more challenging to his ability, but it is not without its difficulties. It becomes necessary to discriminate in order to seek circumstances in which to opt for the ambitious or difficult strokes. If there is the slightest doubt, then the player should take the simplest option, especially if the situation in the match is tense or critical. But there are times when the player must put into practice what he has learnt, create situations to finish the rally, and ultimately win the points.

A good example of this concept occurred in 1980 during a match between Gawain Briars (Great Britain) and Selwyn Machet (South Africa). The situation reached two games all and Briars found himself game and match ball down in the fifth game. He clawed his way back to 7-8 and lost the rally, so Machet came back to serve at match ball. Machet's service landed directly on Briars' racket and he aimed at the cross-court nick from the backhand side. Unfortunately the ball hit the top of the tin and jumped fractionally to make it ball down – game and match to Machet. There was some criticism and not a little surprise that Briars should risk such an ambitious stroke at such a crucial stage. It was perhaps a little impetuous, but nevertheless the philosophical rationale behind what was an error was that the service was of poor quality and that the stroke selected had been practised thoroughly, so Briars had confidence in his ability to make it successfully. Furthermore, his instincts were probably honed by the fact that the poor service should have been despatched by the chosen stroke. The attitude is laudable, but the point in the match at which it was chosen is more arguable. Nevertheless the message is clear: if the winning stroke is an option and it has been well rehearsed, then the player should not be afraid to employ it. At the same time, commonsense must be applied and if the stroke goes wrong and confidence is lost in it, the player should opt for an alternative. This situation emphasises the need for flexibility and the all-round skills this requires.

Under such tactical variance the opponent can never be sure what will happen in the next rally. Squash has now been recognised as not only a physical challenge, but also a mental test, which has merited the description of 'mobile chess'. This particularly recognises the game as a series of moves that are selected by the individual, but have to be completed by the physical capacity to perform them. It is the all-consuming nature of these challenges, ultimately leaving the player on his own using all his mental and physical attributes to overcome an opponent, which is the attraction for many participants.

This book does not aim to be a definitive coaching manual, because at the end of the day the player is on his own in the court. An abundance of ideas should, however, give the reader food for thought and scope for improving his play with new initiatives; but there will not be strict instructions as to how to play. The basic aspects will inevitably leave little scope for interpretation because they need to be mastered in order to provide a sound platform for error-free rallying; but development from this point is by no means stringently dictated and is meant to be open for the individual to progress in his own way so that no two players end up playing in quite the same way. Interpretation of the ensuing guidelines should produce many different ways of doing the same thing. Coaching is here seen as comparable with the underlying philosophy of playing the game – that is, flexibility around some fixed guidelines. It is important to realise that this is by no means the only approach to playing the game and, by the same token, the player should seek as many different views as possible and attempt to assess their merits and demerits. Then he should try to assimilate into his game the aspects that may be of specific value.

There have been frequent suggestions that squash provides poor spectator appeal. This cannot be valid criticism, if for no other reason than that it has enticed those three million or more players, a percentage of whom will always be keen to see the best exponents of their chosen hobby. It has been said that the subtle skills involved in a game of squash are not easily understood, nor are they necessarily a good source of entertainment to the uninitiated. Against these claims must be balanced the fact that at a British Open final, which was played on a four-walled transparent court, there was the largest spectator audience yet of about three thousand people. That suggests that squash does indeed have spectator appeal.

In any sport there will always be a requirement for those who play as a hobby to watch those whose ability has highly developed the skills in which the part-timer is dabbling. Attention will be paid here to some of these aspects and to aesthetic appreciation, because this is how the average player can gain a greater insight into the game as he develops his individual instincts from the basics.

Watching the sport's top players makes the game look easy. But then all top players in every sport have the capacity to make the game look easy. It is the apparent ease of movement in squash, which makes the top player appear to be merely walking around the court, that deceives the audience. It is useful to watch the best players in action against those who are not quite so good, because the comparison of levels highlights the difference in skills. In addition, it will be seen that the lesser player can suffer what looks like a humiliating defeat in relation to the points scored, but has in fact, given a good account of himself.

Alternatively, the sport can be presented as a powerful gladiatorial contest which is particularly relished by its aficionados, and in venues such as the championship court at the Abbeydale Park club in Sheffield the amphitheatre setting is

The perspex court at Wembley Conference Centre. This 'goldfish bowl' is the setting for the modern game – a dramatic evolution from the original masonry box

almost realised. The particular atmosphere at Abbeydale is created by the cosiness and the lack of room for vast crowds, so that when the gallery is full of enthusiasts it seems that they are within a fraction of being on the court with the players. These surroundings add enormously to the tension of the contest. Unfortunately the advent of the transparent courts and their box-like nature, enclosing the players, has meant a loss in atmosphere, but this is a necessity in catering to the needs of a larger audience.

There is no doubt that watching the best players in action is the best way of learning and improving, and aesthetic qualities will be examined with the club player in mind. The first thing that most spectators appreciate is, as in most racket sports, the players' handling of the racket skills – in other words, ball control.

Quite often the flamboyant player will use such skills for the greater entertainment of his audience and select strokes that are both very difficult and highly effective. Such strokes are to be used with discretion, because they may be sufficiently indiscreet to affect the overall outcome of the match in a tournament situation. The ball control will be just as impressive if the player demonstrates strokes such as the straight drive to the back corners which clings to the side wall. Another aspect of ball control, which is greatly appreciated, is the good player's ability to make an accurate return from his opponent's fine stroke. Such ability is also linked with the player's quality as an athlete. Further athleticism is the means by which good players make their strokes look easy and it confers the advantages of poise, good balance, speed, agility and endurance. While the player can work at all these qualities separately, it is the combination of all of them which can turn him into a gifted mover and offer him the possibility of becoming a good strokemaker. The discerning spectator will see squash movement in terms of the artistic, and some players have been described as like ballet dancers in their ability.

This is a far cry from the gladiatorial and animal-like conception of the squash contest, but then there are, thankfully, many different expressions of personality and body types. The spectator will appraise each player in terms of his physical shape and size and this will relate to his athleticism as well. It is unlikely, for example, that a tall, thin player will be described in terms of ballet when he will possibly have a slightly clumsy air and a long reach. Equally the same body type may well have learnt to move in the same manner as a smaller player, in other words, taking short steps to reach the ball. Both of these movement types are equally valid provided that the player is well balanced when he arrives to present himself for the stroke. There is no restriction on players' shapes and sizes, but what is critical is the efficiency with which they move around the court. And as his standard improves, and as endurance and speed become essential ingredients, so the player will need to improve his efficiency of movement.

Efficiency of movement in the best players is usually clearly defined, especially so in one who is not particularly gifted with the right athletic build. Those players who are noticeably tall or large will show in their movement just what can be done in working for greater efficiency. Hiddy Jahan is probably one of the best examples of this. He has always been a gifted strokemaker, but not the most athletic of players. His skill in movement, however, has been so developed that although it never seems likely, he is always in the right position at the right time.

The enlightened spectator, searching to learn and appreciate more about the sport, will study the top players' ability to demonstrate anticipation, ingenuity, imagination and improvisation allied to racket skills and athleticism. These are the tactical skills which make the best players so much better than those trailing in their wake. Invariably this will be categorised as flair or talent.

There are players in recent times who can be considered as having specific talents and this is a good moment to take a brief look at some of them. Qamar Zaman demonstrated a desire to attack the front areas of the court constantly and also had a penchant for the unexpected, as already mentioned. Gogi Alauddin, on the other hand, was a touch player who refused to hit the ball with great ferocity, but would weave a web of lobs, drop shots and angles which more often than not ran his opponent to a standstill. Hiddy Jahan, completing a triumvirate of Pakistanis with differing styles, has probably been one of the hardest hitters of the ball ever, but of particular interest was his ability to flick his wrist and inject incredible power into his stroke with no apparent back-swing or follow-through. This ability deceived most players. The Australian Chris Dittmar, runner-up in the 1984 British Open, is a more recent addition to the ranks of players who are capable of being difficult to read and, as a result, highly successful at making winners. Particularly in Dittmar's

Gogi Alauddin – a highly skilled tactician who was one of the original four players on the professional circuit

*Hiddy Jahan blends violent hitting
with deft touches – a most exciting
player from the spectator's point of
view*

favour is the fact that he is left-handed; unusual, and therefore
more difficult to deal with.

Special mention must naturally be made of the two players
who have dominated the squash world most in recent seasons:
the Australian Geoff Hunt, and another Pakistani, Jahangir
Khan. Hunt has been world champion on eight occasions –
1968, 1973 and 1975-80 – and was twice runner-up to Jonah
Barrington. He has also won the World Open title four times.

Geoff Hunt, ex-World Champion, in action against Jahangir Khan, the current World Champion. These two players have assembled a prodigious array of tournament successes including the World Open and British Open titles

Jahangir Khan has more recently taken over Hunt's mantle, having been world champion since 1981. As well as being runner-up to Hunt the previous year, he has also won the World Open Championship on three occasions. At their best both players demonstrate their supremacy as athletes. That is not to say that they have not been gifted strokemakers, but in the final analysis such has been their athletic prowess and ability to read the game that they have had little need to avail themselves of any extravagant and risky strokes in search of the abundant world titles that they have won between them.

A critical and appreciative eye, then, can play a big part in helping a player to hasten his development. A ready willingness to learn will stand him in good stead in his formative days, and it is hoped that the topics covered in this book will serve as a welcome addition to that process, and also as a further pointer to those players who are eager to maintain the progress that they have already made. The topics covered will be broadly based, and it is hoped that together they will provide perspective, context and objectivity in a sport that can make its players introspective by its very nature. Such introspection is perhaps necessary to achieve the balance of dedication to the sport at the highest levels, but it may in itself have an inhibiting effect on opportunities for broader learning, and there are many of its three million or more players who are more content to enjoy the challenges of squash for their own sake than for such ultimate devotion. We have tried never to forget the interests of the majority when incorporating some details for the few, but instead have aimed to cross-reference ideas at one level of professional playing skill with their relevance to the average player. In that way it is possible to increase appreciation of the skills in the game at all levels. Such a universal accord with squash will only help it to progress further along the road of development and follow the route of other sports, such as snooker, to become *the* game for the next century.

It is for this reason that it is worth considering squash briefly in terms of its development in the more recent past and its changing relevance to contemporary society. As yet it is not a high-profile media sport. But at the same time it is one that many people seem to talk about playing, despite the disparaging comments of a number of club-owners and builders who seem to believe that the bottom is about to fall out of the sport. In their opinion the boom of the 1960s and 1970s is now over, and squash now finds itself in a potentially embarrassing commercial situation. Some are ready to argue that the overall picture will be changed if squash is discovered by television. But it is a sad fact of life that television is still only interested in the sport on a fringe basis, so that lifeline represents only a half-chance. Even so, there is no doubt that the Squash Rackets' Association is trying to tackle the area of the sport's development; they have striven to make progress with particular reference to coaching schemes, tournament schedules, administrative infra-structure and communications on behalf of the players to those people both on the inside and the outside of their world.

Jahangir Khan giving his views for the television cameras. A scene which is becoming ever more familiar as the modern game develops

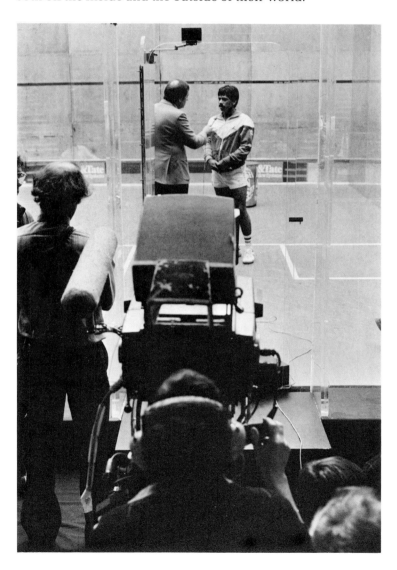

Squash is poised at a stage when the future looks exciting, but there is still much work to be done in creating interest and teaching some of the subtleties of the sport. It has somehow managed to establish itself in the popularity stakes without being highly organised, so as it progresses, there is no telling when and where the next resurgence of interest will emerge. In the meantime, however, it is time to look at the sport as it has developed so far in greater detail, with regard to both objectivity and the specific playing aspects, so that the reader will be able to gauge better just what squash has to offer.

The author entering the world of TV commentating

Hashim Khan – a legend in his own lifetime. The most famous of the Khan dynasty, he always made winning look easy. Here he is seen resting between games at the British Open final in 1985. Hashim found no difficulty in adjusting to the perspex court!

2. The environment of the game

When two players go into the squash court, they take with them rackets and a ball. They proceed to warm up by hitting the ball – so in answer to the question, 'What is a game of squash?', hitting the ball is the prime motive. The layout of the court and the straightforward lines of demarcation govern what is in or out of play. In other words, the line around the top of the court on all four walls designates the area below which the ball must hit the walls. The ball may travel higher than this provided that it does not strike the walls at such a point. The ball must always be struck to the front wall and there is a line on the front wall just above the floor above which the ball must strike the wall.

There is no great difficulty in adapting to the rules so far. As the players move into a more competitive situation, the emphasis is more on extending the rally by one more stroke than the opponent and as the players become more competent, the rallies will be prolonged. This is a purely defensive way of assessing the sport and places emphasis on the player's ability merely to return the ball to the front wall. Obviously there is a way of approaching the exercise with more emphasis on attacking, but this takes practice to achieve. The ball must be struck to tactically predetermined areas of the court and this is a more difficult skill to absorb. It is easier to make mistakes as the player strives to strike the ball closer to the lines in order to increase the difficulty his opponent will face in making his next return. The combination of these two general areas of attack and defence will provide a sensible basic game. Although on the face of it this seems to be a highly simplistic view of the sport, it is worth recalling the advice given by a member of the famous Khan dynasty from Pakistan to an opponent who had been on the receiving end of a rather severe beating and had found himself continually peppering the tin. The Pakistani simply said, 'Hit the ball higher.'

It is easy to look at squash in a simplistic way, but hidden behind this simplicity are areas of greater complexity – mastery of ball control, tactical adroitness, sound temperament, a will to win and finally the relevant fitness quotient. Here we are going to look at these areas, but at the same time attempt to maintain a vein of simplicity running through them.

The simple and methodical approach is by far the most effective and at the outset advice will always be on the basis that if a player is finding something difficult, he should go back to fundamental principles and then try to make progress again. With this standpoint in mind, it is hoped that this examination of the sport will stimulate those who may see it in a different light and not frighten off potential players with thoughts of impossible ball skills and unattainable heights of physical fitness derived from rigorous Olympic-like training schedules. At all times players are encouraged to work towards improving their racket skills, because the racket and ball are the primary sources of fun which attracted them to the sport in the first place. This is the starting point for all players and the object of this book is to try to expand this purpose within everybody's compass rather than to attend purely and simply to the needs of the high-calibre player.

Having entered the court with rackets and ball, the players will then put various attributes and skills to the test to determine who is the better at the sport on that occasion. This competition serves to examine each individual in his mastery of technique and racket skill, shot selection and tactics, temperament and experience, the will to win and determination, and fitness. In later chapters we shall deal more comprehensively with these specific elements, but the player will find that these individual attributes will never be in equal measure and will vary by degrees in each player, therefore ensuring that every new opponent represents a special challenge. The list of qualities mentioned above is in some sort of general order of importance – though others will not necessarily agree with this order. There are, for example, players who place strong emphasis on fitness and would see that aspect as being of primary importance; but in looking to the club player and casual participant, this represents an order that may be particularly significant to their enjoyment.

Technique and racket skills

These are clearly essential, for until the player can strike the ball with confidence on both the forehand and the backhand sides of the court, then he will not be capable of putting together a rally. When he has advanced further, the player must achieve a degree of control over where he is striking the ball so that he has

Qamar Zaman using his skills to keep Magdi Saad of Egypt under pressure chasing a stroke that is well out of his reach. Magdi himself has a similar flair for imaginative shot selection and tactics

Shot selection and tactics

The 1985 British Open Veterans' Final featuring Mohammed Yasin of Pakistan and Ken Hiscoe of Australia, both players with a complete range of strokes. Seen here is Mo Yasin controlling the backhand drop shot to cause the maximum inconvenience to Ken Hiscoe

the facility to hit it out of his opponent's reach, thereby winning first the rally, then the serve and finally the point. Achieving this ability to hit the ball out of the opponent's reach or into a part of the court, such as the back corners, where the opponent will have the greatest difficulty in making good his return, depends on learning the racket skills and working on basic technique.

As soon as the player can control the ball with his racket and strike it where he chooses, he is faced with the next stage of learning, which is to select the various strokes in the right order to force his opponent into the maximum inconvenience to continue the rally. There are two qualities in shot selection that result in good tactics. The first is accuracy and the second is space, whether of height, width or length. The player's prime concern is to utilise these two qualities to the detriment of his opponent's play. In the following chapters we shall consider as many of the variations of the different strokes as possible and

give the player the full range of strokes and tactical options that go hand in hand. There is a tendency to consider merely the play to the back corners, which, allied to fitness and condition, is enough. But this is only part of the story and can be regarded simply as the foundation on which to build a greater range of tactical and stroke-making options. The greater the scope of strokes and tactical possibilities, the more challenging the sport becomes. And while the percentages, without error, represented by back-court and fitness play are admirable in themselves, it is desirable for the player to widen his scope and learn to play sensible percentages, but with a full range.

Temperament and experience

These attributes form part and parcel of the player's individual personality traits and are by and large inherent. They constitute his ability to cope with situations of pressure and to bounce back with a sound and practical response. In other words, it may be the capacity for making good the return of an opponent's near winner with an accurate stroke. On the other hand it may be the ability to keep a clear head and not to panic when the opponent is playing well and has accumulated a useful lead. Players of sound temperament and great experience are able to retain an inner calm and play sensibly as they continue the search for their best form despite the fact that the opponent may, for example, have built up a formidable two-game lead.

Will to win and determination

The elements of temperament and experience are motivated by the player's will to win and equally his determination to overcome any adversity. These two concepts are closely interlinked and are the mental application of the physical stroke-making and tactical decisions. These areas of mental application have the largest bearing on the player's progress and success in the sport. They provide the basis for his discipline with particular regard to his overall potential.

Fitness

Ahmed Safwat of Egypt, a charming exponent of the game's skills over the last decade and more. He manages to conjure up the most exquisite touch on his drop shots and angles, and his pleasant disposition always disguises a strong desire to win

This aspect has different implications for players at different standards, but it should never be underestimated because it is important to realise that squash is a sport which is especially demanding on the body. In view of this, all players must have a healthy regard for their physical capabilities. For the beginner and, more significantly, for the later starter all health warnings should be rigidly observed. For the more regular player it is a question of increasing his physical capacity in all its required forms in order to play the sport more successfully. Each player

will fit into this broad spectrum at some point and will need to attend to his own personal requirements. It may well be best for him to take professional advice from both a doctor and a coach so that he has confidence in his physical capacity. The roles of the doctor and the coach are of paramount importance. In the simplest terms, the coach can devise a squash programme based on the counsel given by the doctor and this can play an important part in helping to allay any fears that the player may have about his condition. From a health standpoint it is always crucial for a player to attain a basic standard of fitness before he plays regularly.

Before considering the more intricate details involved in playing squash, it is prudent first to take a look at the players' equipment in general terms and make some observations. The increased popularity of the sport has focused attention on the manufacturers in tandem with the scientific and technological developers relevant to the player's equipment and environment. These have changed since the early days of squash and they are examined in this context with particular reference to the ball, the racket and the court.

The ball

Research has been carried out on the ball ever since the days when the dot was first implanted into it with differing colours to designate its pace or speed. Furthermore there has been research into non-marking balls and this has subsequently involved different basic colours. So far, however, the balls have been predominantly of black, green or blue. In addition, there have been experiments with other colours purely for the sake of the television cameras. This includes the most recent ball which has been created in the likeness of a golf ball with dimples. This is basically the same ball as normal, except that the dimples have been added, and the playing characteristics are the same. But into these dimples have been placed reflective substances and when these are coupled with a television camera with a special light system, the squash ball becomes infinitely superior for the needs of television viewing. The principle, in fact, is the same as that used for 'cat's eyes' on roads and, just as significantly, the ball remains the same to the players and to the live audience.

When choosing a ball, the player should take into account his own standard and the conditions or temperature of the facilities in which he is about to play. It would be ridiculous, for example, for a rank beginner to use a yellow-dot ball – the slowest of all

Jonah Barrington refers to his most memorable matches as 'brutal battles' and further talks of 'murder on the squash court', both remarks indicative of his fierce determination to win. He is seen here opposed by Geoff Hunt of Australia who was the prime adversary of Jonah's most successful years

and the one normally recognised as the competition ball – because in cold conditions there would be little or no bounce until it had been warmed up. The beginner would find it especially difficult to hit the ball hard enough to make it warm and as a result he would make his process of learning twice as hard.

The tendency with a cold ball is for rallies to become short and somewhat frustrating, and it is even feasible for club players to use a white-dot ball in the middle of winter to create extra bounce and therefore a better game. The normal balls and their qualities are: yellow-dot, very slow; white-dot, slow; red-dot, medium; blue-dot, fast. There is also a ball called the double-dot, which is again a competitive one for tournaments. But above all the player should, where possible, always choose a ball which suits his own needs and he should not be afraid to use it. Obviously in tournament play the specific ball is designated by the rules of the event, but at other times the player should use the selected ball by agreement with his opponent.

The racket

There are many different makes of racket on the market and at the moment there is great interest in the development of the new graphite and composite rackets. This may all be somewhat misleading to the player, and it is sufficient simply to stress that he should look for a racket that feels good in his hand. Furthermore, it should be one with which he feels that he is going to be happy on court.

As in tennis, the graphite rackets are expected to take over gradually. There are some interesting aspects, such as the increased durability (some companies have for the first time offered guarantees of unbreakability), and also the slightly larger head, sometimes called the mid-sized head. The racket companies argue that the larger head will increase the 'sweet spot', which is the area of the racket where the ball and the racket make the best contact for timing and accuracy when the ball is struck. As with equipment in all sport, the racket has increasingly benefitted from the advantage of scientific technology in the progression from the original wooden rackets to the modern graphite composite.

The court

In the same way that the racket has felt the benefit of new technology, so the squash court has encountered more visually impressive change. Originally the court was quite literally made up of four walls of plaster, a roof and a floor in a box shape. But this was improved with the advent of the glass-backed wall, pioneered by the Ellis Pearson company. Such a court provided scope for the number of spectators to be increased to anything between 50 and 250 people. This glass back wall clearly required supporting fins and toughened glass to withstand the possibilities of contact not only with the ball but also frequently with the body weight of a player who is off-balance. Nevertheless, with the technology available, this was the first step towards squash as a spectator sport.

The ultimate development of this concept to date is a portable court with four transparent walls. The walls can be constructed

The 'crow's nest' is the latest innovation to assist the officials who control matches in 'goldfish bowl' courts

of either of two different materials: there is a court of glass made by Ellis Pearson, and the new perspex court which has now been bought by the Squash Rackets' Association. The two courts represent the most exciting developments so far, and include some fascinating aspects, such as the twin-vue properties, the enormous weight and the portability.

In simple terms, the twin-vue characteristics produce a situation in which the spectator can see in, but the player cannot see out. This is achieved by a series of dots set into the materials and activated by implanting bright lighting within the court and ensuring darkness outside it. The twin-vue property is not total, but it is enough for the players not to be unduly distracted while a match is in progress. The walls appear to the players to be somewhere between the colours of white and grey, and for this reason a white ball has occasionally been used to contrast with the greyness of the background; it is also hoped that it will show up better on the television cameras. The weight of the court may be as much as ten tons or even more and this therefore causes problems of portability, but so far this has not hindered its use in England and other parts of Europe.

The cost of this development has been astronomical and consequently there has been only slow progress in the use of these courts. The average club player will be well used to playing on the original style of court or the court with glass back wall, but he will probably have no experience of the transparent 'goldfish bowl'. This is, however, purely because there are at present no such courts built into clubs. By and large the different types of court will have similar playing characteristics, although there will be some differences in the brightness of the lighting, the colours of the walls and floor, the temperature and the bounce of the ball off the walls and floor. It is important for the player to realise that such differences will usually be minimal and that it will take him only a few minutes of warming up to adjust to them.

The equipment, then, is the fixed environment of the player and it is his use of it that gives him the chance to test himsef and his skills against other opponents. It should, however, be stressed that there are insufficient variables in the equipment to offer enough reasons for failure if that should be the outcome of a player's games. The source of improvement is rarely attributable to a new racket or a different ball or court, but to the player's greater work for improvement.

Rules and behaviour

Another fixed characteristic of a game of squash is the rules of the sport. While it is not intended here to give detailed recourse to the rules, it would be remiss not to consider closely some of the areas with which they seek to deal. For instance, there are currently two different versions of the scoring system. These link with the two essentially similar, but still slightly varied, games of squash that are played. On the European side of the Atlantic the majority of players will be familiar with the fact that the soft-ball game, as it is known, is played over the best of five games to nine points and a point is scored only when the player is in hand, in other words, serving. So it is necessary to win a rally before obtaining the right to serve, the exception being, of course, at the start. The essential difference between the soft-ball game and the scoring in the American game is that there matches, by contrast, are played to fifteen points and the best of five games and the points are scored at the conclusion of every rally irrespective of who is serving. Interestingly, the soft-ball version of doubles adheres to the American system of scoring.

Perhaps the greatest area of difficulty in squash relates to the fact that the two combatants are in close proximity and at times share the same space in the court. While they both seek to strike the ball to the same wall, there are obviously going to be 'traffic problems', with the players likely to get in each other's way whether it be accidentally or deliberately. Equally, the most dangerous situation of all can occur when the ball is struck to the front wall and it strikes the player's opponent, which prevents it from reaching the front wall. Obviously there is good provision for these circumstances in the rules, but there is often controversy involved in the way in which they are applied because the specific application is left to the referee's interpretation.

There is another aspect which the referee has to monitor carefully, and that is the health and safety of the two players. The rules concerning lets and penalty points also make provision for the players' safety and a good deal of commonsense is required to prevent the racket and the ball from becoming lethal weapons. One particular form of injury that has occurred occasionally in recent times is that to the eye, since the ball is small enough to penetrate the eye socket. The ball may travel at great speeds, so it is imperative that the players watch it at all times in order that any necessary evasive action can be taken. It is important to remember that provided that the player watches the ball all the time, then evasive action will be instinctive, and will also be of great benefit to him in improving his game. If either player suspects that there will be a risk of injury to his opponent by playing the ball, then he must stop and politely ask for a let ball. In such circumstances no referee will turn him down.

Similarly, when the racket is wielded erratically it can be a source of great danger to the player, and the referee is empowered to issue a warning and take action against excessive and dangerous swing. At some time in their careers most players will receive slight cuts and bruises as a result of a racket swing or crowding in too close to their opponents' rackets. It is always important that such cuts and bruises should remain in the minor category.

Apart from the danger to the eyes, all players will at some stage or another receive the stinging mark of the ball on other parts of their bodies, normally their legs. It is to be hoped that such blows will be accidental, but the referee is again empowered to monitor any crudely aggressive play and take the necessary steps against it.

So far the players' safety has been the particular cause for concern relative to the rules. This is clearly of paramount importance, but it is also necessary to look in broad terms at the difficulties of the 'traffic problems'. Many words have already been written about this area, so only some general observations will be made here.

A squash match is fundamentally controlled by two officials, a marker and a referee. The marker takes responsibility for running the game, that is, calling the score and taking charge of the 'administration'. The referee has the task of making decisions and ensuring fair play, so essentially he is in the hot seat. All appeals should be lodged with him and he has the final say. The referee has three decisions to consider in relation to 'traffic problems' and these are: let, no let or penalty stroke. It is necessary to make one of these decisions so that each player in turn can have access to the ball and a fair chance to make a reply to the opponent's last stroke. Any deliberate interference will be deemed unfair and be severely punished. The spirit of the game places an equal burden on each player to ensure that 'play is continuous' until such time as the rally is brought to an end by legitimate means. It is important for the long-term development of positive play that the players have a healthy respect for this particular area of the rules, because there is nothing more aesthetically displeasing than a match which is ruined by two participants attempting to exploit the penalty point rule for their own gain. It can often be observed that those players who do look for the penalty point do so in order to compensate for their own inadequacies and their inability to construct rallies and finish them. Such players also have a habit of blocking opponents when they have tried to play a safe 'winning' stroke – in other words, they have failed to put the ball away and wish to slow up the progress of an opponent who would like to be swift to counter-attack. This is also in contravention of the rules and will be punished.

It is accepted that not all players will be good at moving to the ball and then, more importantly, out of the way. Allowances must therefore be made, but wilful obstruction to a player's own advantage must be weeded out by the referee. The rules make provision for the flow of the game and allow each player the chance to exploit his racket skills to the full. At the point where all deliberate physical contact is either avoided or penalised, then the game will be happily concerned merely with accidental 'traffic problems', and in this respect squash is in the fortunate position of having scope within the rules for allowing for doubt so that the rally can be played again. Unlike in many sports, the let can be especially useful to the referee, who can admit that he was unsighted or even unsure and require the players to play again. Care should be taken by referees, though, not to use the let as a way of avoiding a positive decision.

The concept called 'turning' is socially unacceptable as a practice. This relates to a player standing on the forehand or the backhand side of the court and following the ball around a back corner before turning to hit it with the opposite stroke. This is most often put to use, for example, by a player who is weak on the backhand side. He will watch the ball in the back corner, hit the side wall, then the back wall, and wheel round to strike it using the forehand. This is dangerous because the trajectory of the ball is usually directly through the centre of the court, which will be the favoured position of the player who last hit the ball. It is normally the gambit of a player who is low on technical ability and is seeking to avoid the backhand, but it has also been known for some players to use this action as a deliberately intimidatory ploy. It is undesirable and in some squash-playing nations a player can be punished by a penalty point, although this is still the exception rather than the rule. Nevertheless it is anti-social and it may lead to a lack of willingness by opponents to play someone who offends in this way. A player needs only to adopt the right mental attitude to avoid the situation, and if occasionally it is impossible for him to avoid 'turning', which it can be once in a while, then the rules make allowances for a let to be played and so remove such problems.

In all aspects of rule procedures the game remains the most important thing and if both players accept that as basic, then it is quite surprising on occasions how free of let some of their games can be. The greater the degree of ball control and tactical shrewdness, the less each player will allow his opponent to get in the way. Ideally, the player would like his opponent to be running in circles around the four corners of the court while his own position remains static and central. Such a situation is not easy to achieve, but it does illustrate the fundamental principle of using the racket and ball to avoid mid-court traffic problems. This has been a simplistic appraisal of what is a highly complex area of interpretation of the rules, but it is also an attempt to furnish the player with a broader perspective so that specific incidents will fit into place with more relevance.

Gamal El Amir – a most colourful player from Egypt who sometimes feels the need to climb up the back wall in his quest to discuss a decision with the referee!

Nasser Zahran – another Egyptian trying to put across his point of view

In keeping with the general vogue of behavioural deterioration, moves have been implemented to give increased powers to the referee along the guidelines of a specific code of conduct. This is a sad indictment of trends in sport in the modern era, but the necessity is obvious. At the highest levels greater emphasis is still being placed on winning, and as a result there are players who are prepared to try everything in their power to find ways of gaining certain advantages. As it stands at the moment, the problem in squash is arguably not as advanced as in other sports, but if trends elsewhere are anything to go by, it will inevitably increase. This mood appears to stem from the motivation provided by ever larger sums of prize money, and club players, who are willing to take heed of any tips that might be available from the top professionals, soon find such habits easy to copy. So the rules and the code of conduct are there in readiness if there should be any sign of the situation deteriorating. It should be remembered at all times that there are many people who have embarked on personal crusades to try to sell squash to wider audiences, and incidents of bad behaviour will not help their cause but will play an overall part in helping to darken the image of the sport.

Finally, the player will want to enter competitions and special events and every different event will have regulations that vary slightly. It is important for the player to realise that when he signs the entry form, he agrees to abide by the regulations, so he can be penalised accordingly despite the fact that they may not be used in the majority of tournaments. These regulations as such may seem to be trivial, but they often relate to such aspects as the timing of matches, the number scheduled to be played each day, the type of ball to be used and the colour of clothing to be worn. It may all seem petty, but such regulations facilitate the smooth running of the event and the player would be well advised to fall in line with them. If he falls fouls of such rules, it will merely undermine his concentration and, although this in itself may not have a disastrous effect, it can make matches harder to win when they are hard enough to win anyway.

The player has now been introduced to the basic equipment and essential requirements; and just as he will go from the changing rooms to the real activity of hitting the ball, it is time now to move on to examine the actual skills involved.

3. Technique

A squash player of any standard needs the best possible foundation on which to build. If those foundations of a player's game are anything less than secure, then a high rate of errors and an overall lack of success will ensue.

With this in mind, allied to the opportunity to define specific technical terms, there need be no apology for defining the basic aspects of technique. In his encounters with various opponents in the game a player will come across certain participants who rely totally on the basic two strokes – the straight drive and the cross-court drive. Although these players will perform with little imagination or flair, it will still be apparent that their games carry a very high degree of consistency, typified in particular by a very low level of errors. So they will play a total game of squash quite successfully, using only the very basics – and, perhaps to the annoyance of others, experiencing a fair degree of accomplishment founded on the virtues of persistence, athleticism and a desire to wait for the opponent to make the error. This pattern of play highlights the need to master the basics before there can be any recourse to the more ambitious and perhaps riskier strokes of instinct and subtlety.

The basic mechanics of stroking the ball are essential to give a player the chance later to select the appropriate strokes and tactics with which to overcome an increasingly high standard of opponent. So in the beginning there are the grip, footwork and the swing.

The grip

The player should pick up the racket in the middle of the shaft with the left hand. The racket face should be perpendicular to the floor and the handle nearest the player. He should go to 'shake hands' with the handle in the right hand. The thumb and forefinger ought to form a 'V' shape on the top of the handle. The remaining fingers should be spread easily round the handle, gripping firmly, but not too tightly.

The most orthodox grip will present the 'V' a fraction to the left of the handle. This grip offers maximum facility for every

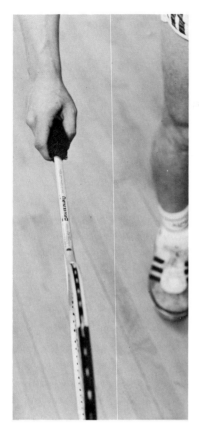

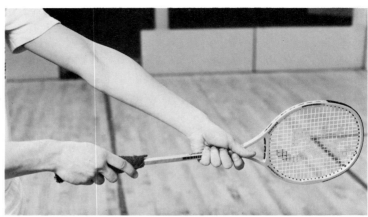

The grip

stroke in the game. Any variations on it may not be disastrous, but might lead to errors at a later stage. Ball control is of the essence and the grip is the start of learning how best to use the racket for this purpose.

It is also important for the player to master the technique of cocking the wrist. The racket will make a 90° angle with the arm when the wrist is cocked and it is essential that the wrist, which contributes to the power of the stroke, should be in this position at the start of every shot. It should remain cocked for every basic stroke except when an opponent has made it impossible and it is necessary to improvise.

Footwork

Good footwork means good balance and that, in turn, gives the player the opportunity to swing the racket correctly so as to produce an accurate stroke. The less body movement there is, other than of the racket arm, the less there is to go wrong with the consistency of the racket swing. Good balance also permits optimum power to be generated. The momentum of the racket swing is transferred from the racket into striking the ball around the pivot of the body's static position. Such balance is achieved by good positioning and that means that the player must be able to play the full range of strokes from a single stance.

The forehand is usually played for all balls on the right-hand side of the centre line to the right-hand wall and the backhand on the left-hand side of the centre line to the left-hand wall. Ideally, the forehand is played with the body turned sideways on to the front wall. The left leg leads and the feet should be approximately eighteen inches (half a metre) apart. The weight should be comfortably distributed between the legs, although probably slightly heavier on the left. The backhand is the exact opposite. The body is turned to the back-hand wall so that its position is sideways on to the front wall and the right, leading leg. Positionally, the same points as those for the forehand apply: they are simply in reverse.

A useful test of balance is for the player to stop half-way through the stroke and ask, 'If somebody pushed me now, would I fall over?' If the answer is 'no', then good balance has been achieved. If not, the player should try to find a more comfortable position.

The player has now been given the ideal balanced position to play all the strokes and, in particular, the drive down the side wall which initially is the most difficult of all. The position, as described, is obviously an ideal and cannot always be achieved, especially under pressure. But it is surprising how often it can be done with practice and it normally leads to a more accurate stroke than one which is hastily improvised.

The swing

Before starting the swing, the player should be aware of his grip on the racket and the cocked wrist action needed throughout the stroke so that the racket face will come through the line of the ball's flight and make the desired contact consistently. It is important that the racket head should remain above the wrist, so the wrist must be cocked before, during and after the stroke.

The swing is one continuous movement which comprises three parts: the back-swing, the down-swing and the follow-through. Fluency and rhythm of swing are essential elements of good ball control and the swing should be consistently smooth because any jerky movement will lead only to error.

Provided that the wrist has been cocked, the back-swing will see the racket raised to the vertical above the head, and it is then that the down-swing begins. The down-swing causes the racket to gain momentum, which is transferred from the racket to the ball at the moment of impact, propelling it to the front wall. The faster the down-swing, the harder the ball will be hit. So that the player can ensure good contact with the ball, the racket head should be travelling in the same horizontal plane as the ball when they meet.

In the later stages of the down-swing the wrist will have started a rotating movement which is completed at the follow-through. The follow-through ends when the racket takes up a vertical position high above the player's head, as if in preparation for the backhand stroke. The whole swing should be full but compact so that there is no danger to life or limb of an opponent who may be close by. The swing should start and finish above the head, which is by and large out of harm's way.

Now that the player has seen how to master the theory of technique required to hit the ball with maximum control, it is time to introduce the ball itself. There are three basic varieties of stroke which are the fundamental requirements for match play: the straight drive, the cross-court drive and the angle.

The straight drive

This stroke, close and parallel to the side walls, is achieved by the player's positioning and then striking the ball at a point where it is level with the knee of the leading leg. He will normally strike the ball at a height somewhere between the ankle and the knee, although it might be higher if the ball is particularly bouncy. Similarly, if the opponent has played an extremely good stroke which is very low, then the player will have to make adjustments to compensate and to ensure a suitably accurate return. The most common adjustment is to bend his knees so that the racket head is kept up. In this way the ball is struck above the tin, not into it, which is a frequent mistake.

It is imperative for the player to practise this stroke as a basic and this may be done without a partner. He should begin by taking up a position at the short line and build up a rally by repeatedly hitting the ball firmly down the wall. This should be continued until the player is inevitably halted by a mistake. He should then pick himself up, dust himself down and start all over again, making a note of the number of successive strokes that he has scored. Wherever possible, he should try to beat his best score each time.

When the player has attained a satisfactory degree of profi-

Backswing, downswing and follow through

ciency, he should retreat to the back of the service box to do the same exercise. Finally, he should retreat further, to just in front of the back wall. The player should hit the ball so that it bounces just in front of the back wall and rebounds from it and then strike it again to the front wall before the second bounce. It is important for him to do the previous routines thoroughly because he will need a warm ball – caused by good, hard hitting or hot courts – for the last exercise. This will ensure that the ball bounces enough to allow the necessary continuity. These practice exercises are the same for the backhand as for the forehand, merely reversed.

The cross-court drive

The player's positioning for this stroke is much the same as for the straight drive except that the point of the racket/ball contact is different. He should strike the ball firmly in front of a point level with the knee, so taking it earlier, before it reaches the body position. The height at the point of strike will be the same as for the straight drive; but it will be necessary to adjust to take into account the bounce of the ball, which will be determined by the opponent's previous stroke.

The cross-court drive is the most commonly used stroke because it is the most natural for a player who swings the racket freely and takes no care with his footwork. As a result, it is also the least effective stroke if it is played badly, as it very often is. It is, furthermore, impossible to practise it alone, so it is most regularly rehearsed in a routine with a partner who will provide the angle stroke to set up the situation.

Once a player has taken up a poor position because of bad footwork, he has only the cross-court drive left to play, so any opponent with a modicum of anticipation will take full advantage of a poor-quality cross-court drive to seize the initiative and ultimately win the rally. So although the technique of cross-court play may be obvious, it is also often neglected, and there are many players who might improve by attending to their basic cross-court drive.

Objectives of drives

The straight drive is a most effective stroke at its best. The target should be for the ball to travel one bounce to the nick at the back wall and ideally the ball should cling to the side wall in its flight. It is virtually impossible to return this stroke, so it is particularly valuable in a rally because, even if it does not win it outright, it should permit a winner to be struck from the next stroke.

The value of the stroke is twofold. It is difficult to return

because the ball clings to the wall and most players will experience problems in trying to return the ball from the back corners. The 'interference' of the side and back walls will normally make it difficult for an opponent to gain the initiative in a rally, so rallies down the side walls will prove to be a good starting-
point for any player.

The cross-court drive is less effective than the straight drive
because it does not have the constant protection of the side and
back walls, since it strikes them at two different points. Its
benefit is that, hit with good width, it will pass an opponent
who is positioned in the middle of the court and force him to
retreat to return the ball out of a back corner.

The cross-court drive should also land at the back-wall nick
after one bounce, but by varying the width the player may make
the ball hit the side wall before it reaches the back wall – or it
may not hit the side wall at all. It is important, though, for the
player to make sure that the opponent is unable to cut the ball off
with a volley from the middle of the court.

The cross-court drive, therefore, is the simple alternative to
the straight drive, and preceded by a service, gives the basic formula for a rally.

If the player's sole intention is to cause his opponent difficulties by burying him in the back corners, then it is at this
stage that the match can begin. This tactic, using just these two
strokes, is sufficient to take a novice to a very reasonable standard because they both present an opponent with problems in
returning them out of the back corners. The position for both
strokes is basically the same so it may not be obvious before the
ball is struck which one the player intends to use, which will
prevent the opponent from anticipating the move with complete
confidence.

The angle

The same basic positioning applies for the angle as for the
previous drives, but this time the player strikes the ball behind
a point level with the front knee. The ball is hit directly into the
side wall, whence it must travel to the front wall to become a
legitimate return. It is necessary to note the geometry involved
in playing the correct angle on the side wall to lay the ball up to
the front wall. Obviously, the angle will vary according both to
the player's distance from the front wall and to the point at
which the ball is required to strike the front wall. Otherwise the
player employs the same techniques for this particular stroke as
for the drives on both sides of the court and he should initially

strike the ball firmly. But there is a tendency to thrash at the ball too hard in the mistaken belief that power alone will put the ball on to the front wall. It is more important for the player to concentrate on driving the ball into the side wall and allowing the angle to throw it up on to the front wall.

Objectives of the angle

In this simple rally which is being built up, the drives deliver the ball to the back-court region, so the angle represents both defence and attack against the effectiveness of these drives. The prime requirement of the angle is that it should make contact with the front wall as low over the tin as possible, otherwise it will set up a kill shot. Clearly, it is perfectly reasonable for the player to attempt this in an attacking situation. But if the player is deprived of time in which to make the requisite preparations and is playing the angle defensively from the back corners, he will frequently use the angle as a means of keeping the rally alive in the hope that the opponent will fail to take full advantage of the poor quality of such a return.

At its best the angle is a potent weapon, but it is often used in too casual and aimless a fashion for it to be anything other than a decided weakness in a player's game. He has little excuse for not playing the stroke at least adequately because it forms a most convenient practice stroke in conjunction with the straight and cross-court drives. Furthermore, it can be practised with a partner, which is significantly more stimulating than the slightly laborious solo exercises.

Position for the angle shot

Practice in pairs is a good means of attaining greater accuracy of stroke, and if the player uses the cross-court drives and the practice partner employs the angle, there should be good continuity. This permits rhythm in stroking the shot with the best possible opportunity for improving the strokes. The angle needs to be hit as low over the tin as possible, while initially the drive should be approximately eighteen inches above the tin so as to deliver the ball firmly into the back-court area.

Using the cross-court drive and the angle should reduce the need for running around in the court and only minor adjustments should be required in the way of movement for position. The crucial factor will always remain the control and accuracy of the strokes. At this stage too much movement will only inhibit the mastery of the stroke and make the footwork more difficult.

The volley

The volley has the same technical characteristics as both the forehand and the backhand drives. The major difference is that the ball is not allowed to bounce before it is struck by the racket. The volley is divided into three distinguishing types.

The first is the low volley. This is played late in the ball's flight and just before it bounces so it is not always easy to play the stroke with accuracy. The second is the shoulder-high volley, which is probably the most frequently played of the three. It is used in the main as a weapon of attack because any ball which can be volleyed at this height is predictably a loose return and the volley, when struck low over the tin, can be the winning stroke. Sometimes it is not convenient to organise a full swing of the racket in this context. As a result, the swing is quite often reduced to a short, sharp punching action to produce what is sometimes called a stop-volley. This usually takes place because a player has insufficient time in which to prepare the full stroke.

The third type of volley is the overhead volley, which is self-explanatory and is the type most commonly used as a counter to the lob. It is a good means of stopping the ball from dropping into a back corner like a stone and dying there, giving the player no chance of making an angled return. Hence it solves difficult back-court problems without the inconvenience of actually playing from those areas. In other words, the ball is being cut off earlier in its flight. Obviously the better the lob, the more difficult this overhead volley becomes, and it is important to have good balance and positional play so as to stretch upwards and still be able to make a good return. If the player achieves a good position from which to play the stroke accurately, then he can by all means aim his return low over the tin. but if the lob should be particularly high and therefore effective, it is a good idea to aim the return unambitiously at a safe height – the cut line, for example – so that it travels to the back-court region. This has the effect of keeping the ball in play with a minimum chance of error.

It should be noted that perhaps the most exciting and extrovert stroke in the game is the cross-court ball to the nick from the lob, usually a less accurate lob return. And it should be remembered that this is not a particularly easy stroke to master although, by its very nature, many players attempt it at a very early stage of their development. The risks are great, both in hitting the tin and in failing to strike the nick, because it presents an easy set-up ball for the opponent. But if the ball should strike the nick and roll out along the floor, then the player has made one of the few certain outright winning strokes in the game. This stroke in particular is one which will respond to extensive practice.

Just as effective but more difficult still is the overhead volley struck low over the tin and straight to the side-wall nick, as opposed to the cross-court. This requires especial accuracy, but it also has its rewards as an outright winner.

So far the volley has been considered as a firmly struck shot and it makes for consistency and therefore accuracy to do so. but the drop shot – a stroke of delicacy and touch – may also be played on the volley. The player should remember, though, that the drop volley works effectively only when his confidence is high. If the player should be lacking in confidence, then the drop volley will be prone to error and should be avoided. Again, at its best it is a particularly lethal weapon and a great source of outright winners.

This completes our survey of the technical aspects of the strokes. Naturally, because the player has been introduced to these aspects of stroke-making in a most general and all-embracing way, the specific aplications of them will inevitably throw up some discrepancies, and so it will always be worth consulting a coach who can analyse and solve individual problems. Nevertheless, the player is now armed with the weapons of a rally and is ready to make a start at playing.

4. Stroke selection and tactics

A rally consists of the technical aspects discussed in the previous chapter allied to specific shot selection in its various forms, which is more commonly known as tactics.

So what is a rally? It begins with a service and continues through an exchange of strokes with the opponent until such time as one or the other of the players fails to return the ball to the front wall. Tactics, on the other hand, are the specific choices of strokes that will, it is hoped, compel an opponent to fail to make good his return of the ball to the front wall. There are several varieties of stroke that will cause an opponent different problems, all of which will contribute in their own way towards making it awkward for the opponent to make good his return of the ball to the front wall.

Service

The service is important for two basic reasons. First of all, the server is the only player who is able to score a point at the successful culmination of the rally, the receiver merely winning the

Phil Kenyon of England all set to receive service

Lisa Opie of Guernsey starts the rally with the service

right to serve. The second reason revolves round what might be termed the time factor. It is the only time when a player has the chance to have a static position, thus ensuring good balance (when off-balance, a player is more likely to produce a poor stroke); it is the only time when a player throws up the ball before contact with the complete selection of strokes, as opposed to dealing with the opponent's previous stroke in the rally; and it is the only time when it should always be within a player's capability to produce an accurate stroke. So a good, accurate serve will hold the initiative for the remainder of the rally.

Rules of service

The player must enter the service box and have a minimum of one foot totally within it. For service the ball must be struck so that it hits the front wall before any other above the cut line and lands in the opposite back quarter. There are two forms of fault: at worst the rally may be lost, but there are situations in which a second bite at the service cherry is available.

There are four ways of losing a rally outright: should the ball hit any wall other than the front first; should the ball hit any wall above the out-of-court line; should the ball hit the tin; and missing the ball completely in trying to serve, which is perhaps the most off-putting example of all.

In three instances a server is entitled to two attempts before losing the rally: should he fail to have a foot wholly inside the service box; should he fail to strike the ball to the front wall above the cut line, but above the tin; or should the ball fail to alight in the opposite back quarter.

It should be noted that if the service receiver chooses, the ball may never reach the floor because he is entitled to volley his return. In this category the receiver may opt to take the fault and continue the rally. But two such faults in this category result in the server losing the rally outright and it should further be remembered that the lines in squash constitute a ball out of court, not as in tennis when the opposite applies.

At the successful conclusion of a rally, the server then goes to the opposite box and continues alternating until such time as he loses a rally. The opponent then comes in to serve and is free to select either service box from which to begin.

Types of service

Unlike tennis again, it is not nearly so easy in squash to win the rally outright with a service. Tactically, therefore, the emphasis is more on gaining the initiative in the rally from the service rather than attempting a winning serve. Perhaps the main object is to prevent the receiver from making an outright winner following the service, and to force him into a position in which he can merely make a weak or defensive return. In order to try to achieve these aims, three types of service are most commonly used: the lob service, the flat service, or the corkscrew service.

The lob service

As its name implies, this is struck high onto the front wall so that it strikes the side wall high up and close to the back wall, dropping to die in the back corner. The essence of the lob service is that it should prevent the receiver from returning the ball with a volley because of its height. The lob service is the most difficult one to use effectively because it demands great accuracy. If it is not very close to the walls, it will provide the receiver with too great a freedom of shot selection for his return. Ideally, the lob service should force the opponent to play a defensive angle to return the ball to the front wall, thereby handing the initiative to the server.

The flat service In exactly the same way as the lob service, this derives its name from the trajectory of its delivery. The flat service has various angles of delivery, but relies mainly on speed and surprise as means of preventing the opponent from having the freedom of shot selection. It can, for example, be aimed at the side-wall nick or directly at the back-wall nick; it can be aimed down the opponent's wrong side as he stands in the middle of the service box (although, at a lower level of experience, it should be noted that this service must be used with care because it causes the opponent to turn on the ball and conceivably strike it back at the server); or it can be aimed directly at the receiver's body, again with the intention of denying the opponent both freedom of shot selection in reply and a chance to take the offensive.

The corkscrew service In order to create the corkscrew effect, the ball is struck high up onto the front wall and close in to the nearest side wall, directing the ball to the opposite back quarter and imparting a spin so that when it hits the opposing side wall, close to the back wall, it will ideally bounce parallel to the back wall and as close as possible to it. The backhand service is required from the right-hand service box and the forehand service is necessary from the left-hand service box so as to give the required angles of delivery. The effectiveness of this service is that it is difficult to volley in return for two reasons: the height line of flight should be hard to judge because the ball should be spinning quite considerably, and, furthermore, once the ball has bounced it should be clinging to the back wall, leaving no possibility of a return. The stroke is lethal when played well, but at the same time it is very difficult compared with other services because of the added distance and the intrinsic angle needed to deliver the ball to the opposite back quarter. As a consequence it is seldom used, and is regarded by professionals as a 'trick shot'.

Return of service

In the same way as the server has time to prepare himself and his stroke, so his opponent has the chance to choose his position in the appropriate back quarter to receive the service, given that it must land in that same quarter. The best position from which to receive service is a central point in the back quarter area, which allows maximum freedom to step forward to volley a poor service which has not hit the side wall. It also provides the option to retreat to play a good service out of the back corner from the back wall.

On making good his service, the server will seek to take up a position in the middle of the court – also known as the 'T' – from which he can seize the initiative for the rest of the rally, thereby ensuring its successful outcome. The receiver must then seek to gain the initiative by playing a stroke which is sufficiently out of reach of the server to move him from the mid-court position, so permitting the receiver to take over that position. The ideal return of service will, then, be the drive down the nearest side wall to the back-court area. It will be more effective still if it is on the volley.

At this juncture the rally can begin to take shape following the return of service and the subsequent varieties of stroke will be possible elements of any one rally, depending, of course, on the players' shot selections. With regard to which strokes should be used, the players will dictate to one another and also try any favourite tactical ploys which, they feel, may be particularly suited to their game. The main body of a rally consists of several fundamental variations.

Varieties of stroke

The fundamental drive strokes discussed in Chapter 3 will form the basis of a rally. For example, the drives – both cross-court and straight – to the back-court area will permit a player to take up the mid-court position. If an opponent should counter with a suitably accurate drive return, then the positions will reverse. But if an opponent makes a weak return, such as dropping the ball in the mid-court area, then strokes by which pressure on the opponent can be increased must be employed for the rally to be won. Such attacking strokes are the kill, the drop shot, angles, or the lob.

The kill The kill stroke starts from the same technical basis as the drive, the difference being that the ball is aimed to strike as low over the tin as possible without hitting it. The kill is often aimed at the nick short from the front wall, although it need not necessarily be. There are players who can stun the ball with such power that it barely leaves the front wall before it has bounced twice, Hiddy Jahan probably being the best-known exponent in recent times. The effectiveness of the stroke is easily grasped by noting the position of the opponent in the back-court area when the ball is in the front-court area. The kill stroke may be played either to the straight side or cross-court and the ball is hit considerably harder than for an ordinary drive.

Lucy Soutter (1985 British National Champion) demonstrates all the aggression of the kill shot, striking the ball hard and low over the tin so that it bounces twice close to the front wall

The drop shot   The legendary Hashim Khan once described the straight drop shot as the most important stroke in the game. Positionally, the drop shot is played in the same way as the drive and the kill. The essential difference is that it is played with touch – that is, without power – and the ball is left stranded in the front-court area because of its lack of pace as well as its lowness. The technical requirement for a lack of power consists of a shortened back-swing, but accuracy must be maintained and the follow-through of the swing must not be neglected, otherwise there will be a tendency for the ball to dribble onto the floor. This is a fre-

Lisa Opie bends her knees to balance herself for the deft touch required for the backhand drop shot. She is watching the ball with great concentration while Robyn Blackwood of New Zealand is preparing to leave the mid-court area on her journey to retrieve a stroke which will remain close to the front wall

quent mistake in the technical use of the drop shot. The stroke can be aimed at two distinct areas – the nick (straight and cross-court) or very low (straight and parallel with the wall or a fading cross-court shot).

Angles

The third means of ending a rally revolves round the angle or the reverse angle. This has a disadvantage over the previous two ways in that the ball has extra distance to travel before hitting the front wall and subsequently dying (bouncing twice). But a slight advantage of the strokes is that they are delayed in the point of strike so that they hold the opponent in suspense before he is able to decide where to go to retrieve. There are two types of angle shot. One is driven sharply into the side wall, hitting the front wall at a point close to the opposing side wall and, with practice, dropping into the nick. The other angle is driven in a more shallow way into the side wall, delivering the ball to the middle part of the front wall and then second bounce to the opposite side wall.

The lob

If any of the three previous strokes should be less than inch-perfect and should, therefore, fail to be outright winners, the lob is the counter-measure to use under pressure, provided that it is played with athleticism, agility and ball control. It is the in-rally use of its service namesake. The essential ingredients of the rescue act which it is seeking to perform are the height, depth and lack of pace – touch – that bury the ball deep in the back-corner areas, so making the return extremely difficult. It must

Gamal Awad of Egypt using an angle of an unorthodox nature in his match with Dean Williams of Australia. Gamal is playing the stroke off the 'wrong foot' and is not actually watching the ball

be made impossible to volley the return of this stroke because a poor lob will almost inevitably spell the end of the rally. The situation is that the opponent's previous stroke will essentially drag the player out of position and the lob will attempt to create time for him first to return the ball, second to regain his balance and finally to allow him to take up the mid-court position himself. Technically, the stroke is perhaps one of the most useful. As well as being used defensively, the lob may be highly effective when used in an attacking context, such as from the mid-court position.

Cosmetic strokes

So far, all the basic strokes which comprise a rally have been discussed, but there is another category of stroke which is more cosmetic than fundamental. These strokes, which tend to marry difficulty with effectiveness, are the corkscrew lob, the skid boast, and the back-wall boast.

Gogi Alauddin uses the lob as a major attacking weapon and is arguably the finest exponent of the shot. His balance, poise, footwork and concentration are all of particular importance

The corkscrew lob   This has largely been considered under the same heading as a means of service, the difference being that in this instance it is being used during the course of the rally. If a player tends to favour the stroke, though, it is important that he should practise it thoroughly before use in crucial match situations because of the technical difficulty involved in playing it well.

The skid boast   This shot is an adaptation of the angle. It is necessary to hit the ball high and rising into the side wall so that it is thrown up high onto the front wall. The skid effect from the side to the front wall is achieved by the use of power. From the front wall the ball travels in the manner of a high lob to the opposite back-court area. The stroke has the characteristics of a lob to the extent that the pace tends to be lost after leaving the front wall.

The back-wall boast   Except in sheer desperation, this stroke should be retained simply for exhibition match purposes. It is a last line of defence when the ball has passed a player and he is facing the back wall, his only option being to hit the ball, usually with a last-ditch flick, in a high and rising direction from the back wall as if he were lobbing it to the front wall. It is, therefore, a form of reverse lob. It is a difficult stroke to play with any accuracy, but it is possible that, on leaving the front wall, the ball will land awkwardly close to a side wall. The stroke has two possibilities.

Under the immense pressure of Qamar Zaman's accurate stroke play, the author is forced to back wall boast the ball out of the forehand back corner. This stroke is to be avoided if at all possible; here, typically, the point was lost as a result of Qamar's reply to the back wall boast

On the one hand it ensures continuity of a rally from a hopeless situation: on the other it may just land somewhere sufficiently troublesome to an opponent for a player to have the chance to re-establish himself in the mid-court area. Just occasionally and fortuitously the ball ends up falling as a winner, but the odds are heavily stacked against it.

Tactics

Now that the player is equipped with the weaponry at his disposal – the variety of strokes and their possibilities – it is time for him to marshal those forces so that he can put them into practice in a more disciplined and organised fashion in terms of winning rallies, points, games and matches. Such organisation takes into account not only the varieties of stroke available, but also the weaknesses of an opponent and the prevailing conditions, such as the temperture of the court. This is commonly known as match tactics or what the Americans might call 'the game plan'. The tactics have to be reviewed in the context of three elements – attack, defence and counter-attack – and are governed by a central theme of position play.

Attack

Attack is derived from a weak return by an opponent and is geared towards applying as much pressure as possible in attempting to win a rally. The main ways of achieving this aim are by the lowness over the tin – with or without extremes of power – the nick or the low ball clinging to the side wall. The end-

Jahangir Khan moves on to the attack, which does not bode well for Qamar

Jahangir Khan, World Champion and the complete player, is just as adroit in defence as he is in attack

product for an opponent is that he must hurry to retrieve the ball, if it is at all possible. When exerted, such pressure causes at worst extremes of fatigue in a player when constantly applied or at best his loss of the rally. There are two types of sustained pressure in attack: one is in the context of a rally and the other is in the context of the overall match. The end-product is the same. The attacker will more or less dominate the mid-court region positionally, while the player under pressure will be chased around the four corners.

Defence

Defence is the attempt to retrieve the damage done by a poor stroke which has been attacked by the opponent. Positionally, it will pose the difficult task of digging the ball out of one of the four corners of the court. Assuming the skills of the attacker, it is quite reasonable to believe that nothing more will be possible than to return the ball to the front wall with scant possibility of an accurate stroke.

Counter-attack

Counter-attack is defined simply as attempting to turn defence into attack. If it is possible to make an accurate return from the attacker's stroke, it will be either by virtue of a less-than-accurate stroke by the attacker or by anticipation, speed of footwork and good racket work by the player seeking to regain command of the rally. A specifically accurate stroke under pressure is needed to remove the attacker from the mid-court area to one of the four corners so that the player on defence can resume the dominating mid-court position.

Jahangir poised for the counter attack. Note the balance and concentration which give rise to the kind of alertness which is feared by the world's best. One of his greatest assets is his ability to read the game situation

Squash has been likened to mobile chess because it has a similar tactical format and incorporates movement, thereby creating total commitment of mind and body. The game is concerned with manoeuvring an opponent mainly because it is nothing like as easy to make outright winners as it is in, say, tennis. A rally, therefore, usually concludes with a player out of position and the ball being struck into the relevant opening.

Chess is the manoeuvring positionally of an opponent – in other words, his weapons – so that he finds himself in an indefensible position: checkmate. Hence he is the loser. In much the same way squash is based on such abstract manoeuvring. Tactically, chess and squash may be compared. And the single most important ploy to remember in squash is that the ball should, as often as possible, be struck to the corner of the court furthest from the opponent's position.

The way in which a player can manoeuvre his opponent to the best advantage is by his use of tactics, which contain the elements of attack, defence and counter-attack. It is by these means that a player sets out to win the rally, the points, games and the match.

The specific course that each rally will take is going to be predetermined to some extent by the strengths and weaknesses of the strokes in a player's repertoire and also by those of the opponent. The tactics of a rally are inevitably the struggle for ascendancy originating from both players' desire to play to his own individual strengths and to expose his opponent's weaknesses. The whole tone of the match is obvious from the similarity or otherwise of both players' strengths. For example, two players who favour hitting the ball to the back-court areas and waiting for the other to make errors will largely be involved in a long and protracted struggle. On the other hand, two players of contrasting styles – in other words, strengths – may well produce a far more colourful and exciting game.

Positional play

As already mentioned, tactics are governed by the respective strengths and weaknesses, but there is a good axiom for player to bear in mind from the start of a rally: always try to hit the ball to a part of the court where the opponent is not. If the player can strike the ball into the open spaces, then the opponent will be forced to do all the chasing to return it and the middle of the court will then be dominated. As a general guide, the player who commands the middle of the court for the longer period of time will tend to become less tired than his opponent and have the better chance of winning the match. The player who has to chase around the four corners of the court to return the ball will encounter tiredness more quickly and eventually the situation will make it more difficult for him to play accurate, error-free squash. Except in particularly one-sided matches, a player will face periods when he has domination of the court and periods when he will find retrieval in the four corners necessary. When

Geoff Hunt and Ian Robinson. These two shots illustrate good positional play by the player who has forced his opponent out of the centre of the court to the side wall in order to make the return. Clearly two well-matched opponents!

(Opposite)
Jahangir Khan in action against Hiddy Jahan of England. Characteristically, Jahangir is dominating the rally in the middle of the court whereas Hiddy is forced into running around him to the four corners of the court

two players are evenly matched, there will be a constant struggle to return to the central position after every stroke, and a general pointer as to the course of a match can be gauged from noting which one is spending more time dominating the middle of the court.

Once a player has taken the middle of the court, he can stay there only if he is able to play his next stroke into space and to ensure that his opponent has insufficient time to do anything except chase after the ball, without the opportunity to make a good return. As the opponent is dragged into space and his returns become inaccurate, it then becomes easier for the player to anticipate them.

The squash equivalent of a cat-and-mouse game gradually unfolds, for the player will then make an early attack on any weak return, hoping to strike the ball into more space so that the opponent, having been manoeuvred out of position, will be unable to catch up with the ball as it disappears into the other spaces of the court. Manoeuvring the opponent is all based upon the

desire to dominate the middle of the court because it represents the most advantagaeous position from which to play accurate and attacking strokes.

From the outset this positional play is derived from playing accurate strokes which remove the opponent from the middle of the court. It is hardly feasible for two players to play in the middle of the court at the same time and there are rules intended to avoid any obstruction, either accidental or deliberate, in the movement of the players round the court.

Strengths

Every player has his favourite strokes with which he is able to win rallies with confidence. It is important that he should recognise these strokes and structure a rally towards them, because he will then have ready access to scoring points more easily. At the same time the pressure will mount on the opposition and may cause unforced errors as well as those born out of the good strokes. It is sensible to use these strokes as often as possible provided that the situation is appropriate. However, it should be remembered that errors can result from trying to manufacture opportunities to play these strokes in an inappropriate situation.

Similarly, the opponent will have his own favourite strokes and the player must seek them out as soon as possible, so as to steer the rally away from giving the opponent the oportunity to maximise the return from such strengths. For example, the player may well be strong on the cross-court volley into the nick and any ball at shoulder-height would provide the opportunity to play the stroke, so the player would actively seek any chance to score points with this stroke; but if this is one of the opponent's strengths, then the player should be at pains to avoid feeding the stroke by hitting the ball low or much higher.

Weaknesses

Bryan Beeson, a surprise finalist in the 1984 British National Championships, dominates a rally with the eventual champion Geoff Williams, who finds himself for the moment in a position of decided weakness

Just as every player will have strokes that are his strengths, so will he have some that are areas of weakness and a source of errors in his game. The most common example of this concerns the time when a player has just started playing squash. Initially there will be weaknesses in his backhand stroke, while the forehand will be easier to master because it is more natural. In this rather basic example it would be prudent to attack to the opponent's backhand to try to force errors that would lead to winning points. A player must always seek out the weaknesses of an opponent to exploit them to the full as soon as possible.

Another common area of weakness is in the back corners, and it is to these areas that most opponents prefer to launch their attacks. This is mainly because the stroke to the back corners often sets up a loose return from which to finish the rally, if it is not an outright winner in itself. But generally, as standards improve, all weaknesses should diminish to such an extent that they can be measured more by an opponent's inability to win points, rather than by the preponderance of errors that are likely to lose them.

Stroke selection

This is an individual concept simply because it involves each player's strengths, weaknesses, personal preferences and personality traits. There are, however, some guidelines which represent a sound platform for the player's tactical thinking. Because of the general terms in which they will be explored, these give the player plenty of scope for personal interpretation.

The assumption first is that the player has served in such a way that the opponent is unable to make an attacking stroke as a return. The player will then be able to move to the middle of the court and await the return from the backhand corner, since it is assumed that the first service will have been directed at this flank. The return of service has not been good enough for the server to have exchanged the middle of the court with the receiver. From these positions the server's stroke selection can be reviewed. There are three further corners of the court where the opponent is not. It then has to be assumed that the player has the ability to make the stroke to these three corners, although the front corners represent more difficulty than the back. In this instance the short strokes with the opponent at the back of the court may finish the rally: aiming for the opposite back corner will make him hurry, but it is less likely to end it.

As a player gains more experience of match play, he will be able to assess situations more quickly and will find it easier to select a stroke which keeps his opponent under pressure by hitting for the spaces. All the time the player must strive to cultivate an extra sense that will inform him of his opponent's position, so that he can quickly select the stroke which is going to inconvenience him most.

Another factor to be considered is the difficulty of the selected stroke, and if the player has any doubt as to the successful outcome of playing it, then it may well be prudent to pick a safer option while still searching for the space. If he has any reservations about which stroke to select, the drive to the back corner and clinging to the wall is always a good bet because it is difficult for the opponent to attack.

As the rally progresses, the player should play every stroke on the merits of his opponent's last stroke while always seeking the spaces in reply. This should become easier as the player gains more experience. Usually, however, if the player is attacking from the middle of the court, there are many options of stroke selection open to him and these simply have to be produced in the correct order to outmanoeuvre the opponent to defeat.

Stroke selection is more difficult if the player is on the defensive or away from the mid-court position, because then it is frequently only possible to keep the ball in play in order to survive, and selection, apart from the obvious, is out of the question. Ideally the player must select the stroke that leaves the ball as far away from the opponent in the middle of the court as possible. This should force him to vacate the middle and afford the player the opportunity of taking it over. It sounds much easier than it ever is to hit the ball accurately out of the opponent's reach and into one of the corners, because it will always drop into the middle of the court if the player should make a loose return.

In defence the deep, tight straight drive to the corner is the best base from which to work, but if the player has the confidence it is wise not to be totally predictable and to try to vary the returns. Accuracy is a means by which the player can occupy the middle of the court, but it is not always so easy under great pressure. In addition, a penchant for the unexpected is good although it depends entirely on the player's ingenuity. What he must not do is to return the ball to the middle of the court. That will add to the pressure and is likely to result fairly quickly in the loss of the rally.

Deception

The player will find that an opponent at a good club standard with a reasonable degree of athleticisim will be able to retrieve a fair number of strokes, so it will be necessary to add the ingredient of disguise and deception. There is no great mystery attached to this art and gradually it comes to be a natural part of most players' games. The key is to have a good mastery of technique, since this will give the player a greater range of strokes from the same sitaution. To become a master of disguise, the player must try to create the impression that he is about to play one particular stroke, but then play another completely different stroke. The most important aspect is for the player to make the final direction of the ball the direct opposite from the one that

Deception: Qamar Zaman clearly masks his intention with this stroke–from the picture it is nigh on impossible to identify it. It is to be hoped that his oponent has more idea of where the ball is going

he indicated at first. If the two directions are similar, the opponent will find that he can adapt sharply and still return the ball.

For example, the player may appear to prepare for the straight drive at the front of the court, but very late choose to use the short angle. The reverse is also effective, but is more difficult because the straight drive will require power to direct it to the back court. In another instance the player can use the straight drop shot disguise until he hears the pounding of feet to the front corner, but then at the last minute decide to turn the ball across court. This is particularly satisfying when employed successfully and is a favourite trick of the Pakistani players. Deception can also be used from the back corners by a player indicating that the ball is to be driven fiercely down the wall, but then playing the angle at the last moment. This will leave the ball in the front court when the opponent has anticipated a return to the back corner.

There are many variations and it is for the individual to decide which disguises best suit his needs and which he is able to play most successfully. This is when the player has the opportunity to display his own personality and imagination by injecting some colour into his game.

The player has now been guided through a range of possibilities that can help him make the best use of the strokes in his armoury. He now needs to consider how best to work to perfect the techniques of taking full advantage of the options at his disposal.

5. Practice routines

Every squash player, no matter what his standard, will need to engage in a schedule of practices if he is to improve. There are two basic considerations: first, to practise and improve technique and, second, to practise and improve the construction of rallies – that is, tactics. The two can and frequently will be closely interrelated.

The most obvious way of practising all the skills inherent in a squash match is to play a practice match, without all the pressures and tensions that a big match in a tournament provides. Such a practice match will give the player every opportunity to improve his skills and discover alternative ways of winning rallies. However, this does not necessarily provide sufficient discipline to force the player to amend what may already be a poor quality of stroke or bad tactical stroke selection. It is necessary to isolate such failings and to work specifically on these weaknesses in a different situation.

At the outset a partner is essential to create the various returns to give the player the opportunity of practising a stroke in isolation. It need not be assumed that no benefit will accrue to the partner in a practice situation, for there is a high degree of skill involved in feeding the player with the appropriate ball for his practice stroke, and in some cases the routine can be treated as a competition for both players' accuracy.

There is also a role for the coach, who, by his very nature, should be a good feeder and able to require high standards of technical and tactical accuracy from the player. In a situation in which two players do practise together and one player is feeding the other, then obviously they will alternate in order to give both the opportunity to do the practice. No matter which of these situations is utilised, it is important that a player places a high regard on discipline and accuracy during his practice. It is better to go for a practice of high quality than it is to exhibit great quantity. The better the player, the more demanding he will be of himself in the practice situation, and he will, furthermore, not miss any opportunity to put in an extra session. With particular regard to squash – although the equivalent will apply in most sports – there is no substitute for the hours that are spent hitting the ball in the court, provided that perfection is the ultimate goal.

There are various categories into which practice exercises can be fitted.

Static practices

These stem from the original point of hitting the ball and at the outset solo work can be very useful, but it can also be the least fun. There are, however, three routines which are most helpful.

The first routine involves hitting into the service box. A player stands at a position close to the forehand side wall and just behind the service box. The method is to strike the ball to the front wall and bounce it in the service box before repeating the stroke. The aim is to create accuracy and consistency in striking the ball to the front wall so that it lands in the service box as often as possible without breaking the continuity. Initially, a target of ten repetitions should be attempted. Then the player should build his score as high as he can, constantly trying to set new standards. He should note the varying heights and pace at which the ball can be struck to achieve the same target. For example, a hard and low drive will bounce in the box just the same as a high and softer shot, and it is in the interests of the player to learn the differences. This exercise applies to the backhand just as it does to the forehand.

For the second routine the player should repeat the concept

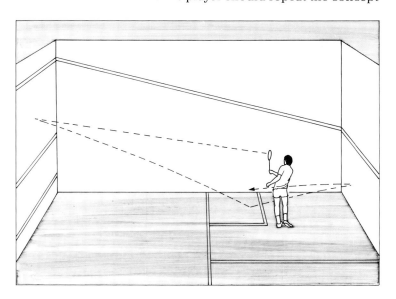

Static practices – hitting into service box

of the first exercise, but this time he should ensure that the ball bounces in front of the back wall, hits it, and rebounds before being struck to the front wall again. This is more difficult because the ball has to travel further from the front wall to reach the back wall, but it has the important advantage of teaching the player about the nature of the bounce of the ball from the back wall. The player should again count the number of successful strokes and should constantly search for his personal best score. This also applies to the backhand and the forehand.

The third routine involves volley practice. The player should take up a position close to the forehand side wall and in the service box. He should then set up a sequence of shoulder-high volleys close to the side wall. The player is again looking for a high number of successful strokes, but if he should find it difficult to master the exercise, then he can move up the court closer to the front wall until such time as he can build up a good score. At this point he can retreat and keep retreating to create difficulties of distance from the front wall, and he should continue to do so as his skills become greater. This routine can also be used for the backhand.

A further adaptation of this exercise involves the player taking up a position in the mid-court area. A forehand is volley-driven cross-court and high up to the front wall close to the side wall, so that the ball corkscrews across the court back to the player, who then volleys from the backhand cross-court high up to the front wall in a similar kind of way.

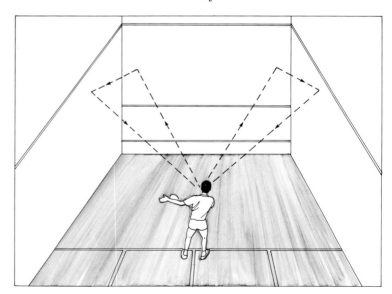

Volley corkscrews

The method of this routine requires continuity of alternating a forehand cross-court volley with a backhand cross-court volley and also an accuracy of stroke, which uses the bounce from the front wall to the side wall to throw the ball back to the player in the middle of the court. This is not an easy routine and it does require some experience of the ball bouncing from the walls. If at first it is difficult to obtain continuity, then, for the sake of understanding what is required, the player can strike the ball lower for this exercise so that he achieves success off the bounce rather than on the volley.

This is an exercise which some professionals will use for show in exhibition matches between games or when they are warming up, but it is fundamentally a very good discipline. So far solo practice is essential in all that has been considered, but a partner or a coach may be added to the formula in order to take it a stage further.

Practices involving slight movement

The scope of practices is limitless in this category, provided that the first player plays a stroke which it is possible for the other player to return to the same area of the court from which it has just been struck.

One example involves the cross-court drive/angle. The first player will set up a backhand angle to his partner's forehand front corner. From there the partner will practise his cross-court drive. The players must have clear definitions of what they are attempting to practise. For example, the cross-court drive must

Cross-court drive and angle

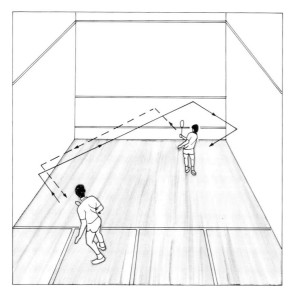
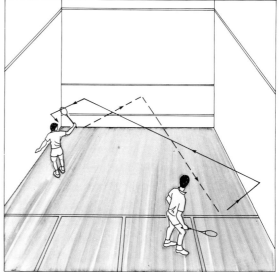

be played either to an area wide of the mid-court or 'T' position, aimed for the side wall at the back of the service box, or slightly straighter, aimed directly to the back corner. The player must also make it clear whether the stroke is to be a cross-court drive hard and low to die in the back corner, or the cross-court kill, which must die before it crosses the mid-court line.

There is a further alternative to this practice, which entails using the cross-court lob, again hit high and wide and caressing the side wall as it drops like a stone into the back corner. The lob requires no pace, but needs a touch that will ensure that the ball will not bounce out of the back corner.

The player who is using the angle has two possible targets. One is to hit the ball low over the tin so that it strikes the front wall in the middle and bounces twice before reaching the opposing side wall. The other possibility is to hit the ball to the three-wall nick by driving it at a steeper angle to the side wall, thereby striking the front wall closer to the opposing side wall and dropping first bounce into the nick.

The players must have a clear idea of what their intentions are to be before seeking to achieve them. It is difficult to turn this into a competitive exercise, except that it is possible to score winning points by hitting the ball to the nick so that one player finds the stroke irretrievable. In this instance points may be scored and some competitive challenges offered. At the same time this exercise is perhaps more useful as a warm-up for rhythm and accuracy rather than for competition.

Another good example of a practice involving some movement involves the straight drive/drop. This routine essentially involves one player to feed and is concerned with positioning down one of the side walls. There are two phases to this: first, the player at the front employs either the straight drive or the straight kill and, second, the player behind employs the drop shot off the straight drive and the feed with little pace and some height – about eighteen inches above the tin – off the straight kill.

This is very much a practice in which the two players co-operate to give each other the chance to practise one stroke at a time, ensuring that they alternate so that they both have opportunities to test themselves. This category of routine can also be adapted to practise the lob and volley down the side wall, the player in front being the volleyer and the player behind using the lob. Again, the lob should be employed to complement the volley rather than to test it.

A further adaptation of the straight lob/volley is evolved when the player in front plays the lob and the player behind makes a volley low over the tin. At this point the degree of difficulty has increased and the player in front must ensure that he is not in the line of fire from the volley emanating from behind. As a result, he needs to return to the mid-court area in order to allow his partner room for some inaccuracy. It may be that either player has a doubt about his ability to practise such strokes without the serious danger of hitting the opponent with the ball, but it is important to realise that this is only practice and that there should be little in the way of competition other than to find a means of producing the most accurate stroke possible.

A further example of practice with slight movement centres round the cross-court lob/cross-court nick. This is based on the previous straight practice, but is adapted to the cross-court. In particular it requires the accuracy of the cross-court volleyed nick. The cross-court lob should then be played with regard to its being of a height that can be volleyed because, played at its best, the lob should rise above the opponent's volley. The cross-court nick is never an easy stroke, but when it is played well it is an outright winner because the ball will roll out along the floor-boards from the nick. It is a spectacular and truly effective stroke, but it does require plenty of hard work to perfect.

This exercise can equally be practised on the volley or off the bounce, both forehand and backhand, and the feeder should afford the player every opportunity to play the nick from most of the positions on the court. At a time when the player derives great satisfaction from playing the stroke with confidence, it is one that can also incorporate the element of surprise if he is happy to play it from less predictable areas of the court.

There can be many combinations in which to practise pairs of strokes and a player can have fun and show a fair bit of imagination by searching for other possibilities that would give practice possibilities, as long as it is remembered that clear definitions of the prime objective of the practice routine must always be a priority.

Practices under pressure

The practices so far have dealt with little more than producing the strokes correctly and accurately, but in a match situation the ball is unlikely to be fed to a position for the player to have the best chance of producing his best stroke. With this in mind, pressure can be created in a practice situation by requiring the player to move varying distances before hitting the ball. Move-

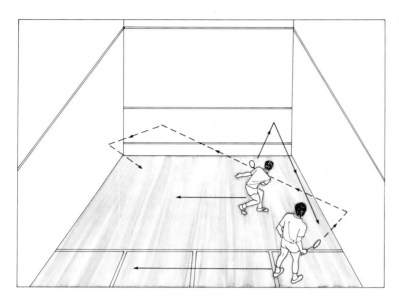

Straight drive/angle

ment to the ball and preparation of the stroke are never easy, particularly when the player is deprived of time by the opponent's good stroke, but there are practice exercises which will help the player to cope with the pressure situations of his matches. At the outset these routines, which become individually more complicated, will be straightforward so that the player can acquire the skills before the heat is turned on and the pressure increased.

Straight drive/angle

This is the most commonly used training exercise and also perhaps the most misunderstood. The aim is for the strokes to be played accurately and both players will alternate between the forehand and the backhand by the very nature of them. The accuracy required will create difficulties of movement and difficulties of playing the subsequent stroke with control. As usual the angle will be aimed low over the tin, either to drop from the front wall into the side-wall nick or to bounce twice before reaching the opposing side wall. The drive, on the other hand, should bounce for the second time at the back wall, although it is no bad thing for the player who is practising the drive to vary the height and power of his stroke provided that he maintains the accuracy. The players will alternate between the drive and the angle.

Cross-court – straight drive/angle – straight drop

This is an extension of the straight drive/angle, but requires greater degrees of control and accuracy to make it effective and is therefore an excellent routine. By introducing the straight drop feed, the player will cause a greater degree of pressure on

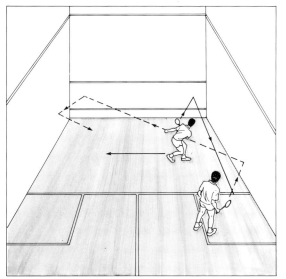
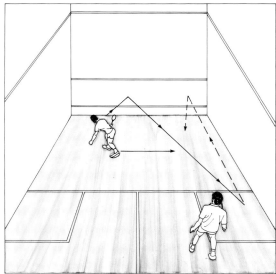

Cross-court – straight drive/angle straight drop

Straight drop – cross-court lob/counter drop – angle

Cross-court lob/straight volley drive/angle

his partner, who will be required to respond with a cross-court drive to the angle and the straight drive to the drop shot. The player will then remain static to concentrate on his accuracy, while the partner will be under pressure to make his drive, provided that the former maintains good control. All the variations which apply in drive and angle may be applied in this instance. The important consideration is for the players to develop rhythm and control over their strokes until they are both satisfied. Again the players will change places after a useful working period of time.

The exercise leaves one player static while the other covers much of the court and experiences the feeling of playing strokes under pressure. The static partner is predominantly a feeder because the practice would scarcely be possible if he played the strokes indecisively. The two strokes to be played by the static partner are the straight drop shot and the cross-court lob and he should use his judgement in placing the ball just out of reach to give the other player a good work-out. The counter of straight drop and angle should be played for ultimate accuracy because this is a tiring exericse and if the strokes are played perfectly, then the feeder will need to stoop to pick the ball up as it hits the nick! Again the roles should be reversed from time to time.

This exercise consists of the alternation of the players through the three strokes mentioned. The player starts by playing a backhand cross-court lob and the partner responds by drive-volleying the ball so that it rebounds from the back wall after the

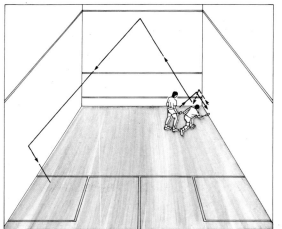

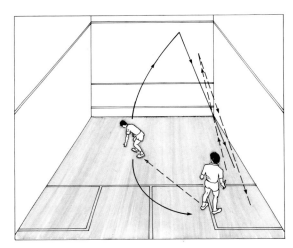

(top left and right)
Straight drop – cross-court lob/counter
drop – angle

(right and below)
Cross-court lob/straight volley
drive/angle

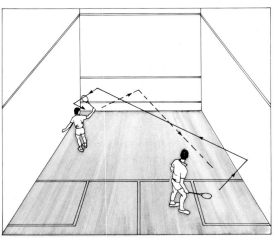

first bounce. The player then plays the angle from the forehand back corner and the partner moves to the front backhand to play the cross-court lob and so continue the rotation. This is an especially useful warm-up exercise because both players experience constant movement. Accuracy of stroke is necessary to create continuity. The players will change sides merely by starting the exercise from the forehand side with the cross-court lob, and then the volley and angle will be from the backhand.

As a general note, these exercises involve a good deal of movement, caused by the necessity for accuracy of stroke, and the players should always bear in mind the value of good movement and balance to cause accurate stroke-play. All the above exercises are designed to capture the practice for movement and stroke-play together.

The three-player practice

Many of the exercises described under the guise of practices involving slight movement can become pressure practices by increasing the accuracy of the feed and sometimes its power. However, pressure can be dramatically increased with the involvement of three players in a double-feed session – in other words, two feeders feeding two separate balls in rotation.

The two feeders stand in each service box and feed the balls alternately, but timed so that the player can move from side to side to practise the stroke accordingly. The feeders' timing with one another is of paramount importance and the type of feed should be a mirror image. The feeders can increase or decrease the pressure on the player by allowing more or less time for the player to move across the court. The balls should be fed to pre-arranged points of height and distance to the front court, enabling the player to practice the same stroke on the forehand and backhand sides.

When the player makes a mistake or hits a poor-quality return, then the feeders must collect the ball again as quickly as possible so that they are ready to feed again and not lose the timing of the practice delivery. It is the sole responsibility of the feeders to provide the situations for the player to practise. At the same time it is the player's total objective to do nothing other than practise the required stroke on both sides of the court, with particular concentration on the difficult movement to connect the two strokes.

There is a great art in feeding the ball accurately for the player to practise and all players will rotate in a double-feed session so that there will be two periods of feeding for one practice routine.

The practice period can be specifically timed, or alternatively a coach or a feeder can monitor timing. This formation may be used to practise any number of different strokes which travel down the walls; but no matter what quality of stroke the player produces, it is the job of the feeder to recover his ball and serve it up to the player in the correct timing.

At the outset the player will be detailed a specific stroke to practise and he will do so intensively both on the forehand and the backhand for the period allocated. The strokes may include the low, hard drive to the back corners and the straight-nick kill, both off the bounce, and the volleyed drive to the back corners and the volleyed straight-nick kill. The lob is also available for such a practice, but the drop shot is better if the feeders move forward in the court, put down their rackets and feed by hand. In the same way the feeders can hand-feed for a volley drop.

The players can put together a good session by practising all of these strokes separately, but eventually combinations of two and three strokes can be put together. For example, the drop shot can be followed by the drive to the back corner and also the lob. The player can systematically work the three strokes in that order or a specified order. All the time the strokes down the forehand wall will mirror those down the back one. Finally, the player can be given the opportunity to mix the various options open to him, which is particularly interesting because it taxes the feeders' abilities to the limit as they scurry up and down the length of their side walls, trying to keep their feeding timed correctly.

The objectives of the double-feeding session are to put the player under pressure to test his movement and to give him the chance to work at his ball control capability under pressure. The movement to the front two corners and back to the mid-court area is difficult when a player is also trying to hit accurate strokes. Obviously the less time that the player has to effect the movement and make the stroke, then the more difficult the stroke becomes and the more prone to error he becomes in executing it.

The double-feed session highlights this difficulty and provides the player with the chance to practise an isolated stroke in these extremes of pressure. It is rare in a match situation that the player will have to respond to more pressure than that which can be applied in this practice situation. Because of the intense concentration and workload involved in this practice, the player will not be able to sustain it for a lengthy period of time. If he is able to do so, then it means that the feeders are not doing their job properly. In a session of double feeding it is helpful for the player to receive encouragement from his feeders. They are usually in the best position to dictate the tempo of the feeding and the duration of the practice, because it will become patently obvious to them when the quality of the player's work has deteriorated because of fatigue. The feeders should not hesitate to call a halt, temporarily at least, if the player can no longer sustain the quality workload once he has been asked for a final burst of concentrated work.

This type of practice requires a high degree of proficiency, both to cope with the intense pressure of the work and the skills of feeding as the players rotate between their respective roles. It is therefore important that the technical ability of all the players involved should be of a similar standing.

As far as ball control attempted in the practice goes, there are three areas of concern. One is the player's attempt to make the ball cling to the side wall. Second, the player should attempt the lowest possible stroke over the tin without actually hitting it and also aim for the nick on the straight side, which is especially difficult to hit. Finally, the player should try to explore the height and pace relationship of a ball struck to the front wall to obtain depth – in other words, getting the ball to bounce in the back-court area.

In this type of practice session it is particularly important for the player to maintain strict discipline and work through the three phases of double-feed practices, attempting to achieve specific objectives from each exercise. The three phases are the single-stroke emphasis, the combinations and finally the mixture and variety of stroke. Their benefits increase the scope for moving towards practice work that more readily includes the cutting edge of a player's competitive instincts.

6. Match practice and the working model

The player is now moving into a match situation and, armed with the experience of the various elements that he has learnt in practice, he is ready to take on the competitive aspects. There is nothing better than match play for improving a player's standards. All the practices that have gone before merely simulate isolated aspects of match play and the ultimate test is found only in the real situation.

Tactical awareness can also be improved only in a match situation because it calls into play the player's temperament and what happens to him in pressure situations. For example, is the player prone to simple errors, in particular at nine-all in the fifth and deciding game? If that is the case, then only frequent exposure to such a situation will make him better at coping with it, so the transition from practice to match play adds the essential ingredient of tactics. However, before moving specifically into match play, there are some conditioned games which are the final vestige of practice and are more geared to competitive match play and the accompanying tactics than to practice.

Conditioned games

These are played with specific conditions that seek to isolate specific strokes. They take on the aspect of competitive play with points scored and games won, but the conditions insist that the targets are certain areas of the court. Such conditions can be employed by the partner as well, or alternatively the partner can take on the role of straight man and contunue to play normally without restriction. The decision as to whether both players play to the conditions or not is usually dependent upon the player's partner. If the two players should be of similar standards, then it would not be inappropriate for both to play to the conditions; but if the partner should be of lesser ability, then it is just like handicapping the player of a higher standard by giving him specific conditions. For the purposes of exploring the various conditioned games, it will be assumed that the player is being handicapped while the partner plays the straight man and, therefore, normal squash.

The back-court game

The player is allowed to hit the ball only to the back-court areas and this can be achieved by setting the marker as either the service line on the front wall or the mid-court line on the floor. In the case of the service line on the front wall, the ball must be struck above that line and, obviously, below the out-of-court line. In the other alternative, the mid-court line on the floor must be cleared as the ball travels to bounce behind it. The handicap for the player is apparent: his partner has to guard only the back half of the court and knows constantly the area into which the ball will be hit.

There are two aspects with which the player must concern himself: first, that he plays his strokes accurately and makes it difficult for the partner to attack him and, second, to see if he is able to explore new areas of the court which he can attack and which he would not normally consider when he has the whole court in which to play. The player will be surprised by the new possibilities of which he will become aware by restricting the area into which he may hit the ball. Hopefully, the end-product will be that he takes this information into a match situation. The player must, incidentally, consider all the available stroke possibilities which satisfy the one criterion of the back-court condition. For example, such a condition does not rule out the angle, but it must be employed as a skid boast, landing the ball in the back court. On the other hand, the drop shot is obviously not possible.

The short game

This is the reverse of the last condition: that is to say, the ball must land in the front part of the court, defined either by the cut line on the front wall or the mid-court line on the floor. The ball must then land below the former or in front of the latter. The short game naturally contrasts with the back-court game since it is concerned with delivering the ball low and to the front of the court. It is a more attacking situation in comparison with the more defensive back-court game. The virtues of height and width are essential to the back-court game, while width and lowness over the tin are the virtues of the short game. Both of these conditions allow for experimentation with combinations of strokes that have rally-winning potential. It has, however, to be said that the nick may be the target with a greater degree of success in the short game than in the back-court game.

Side-wall games

In this routine the area of restriction is that made by a rectangle that extends through an imaginary line from the front wall to the back wall, which is an extension of the line on the outer edge of the service box. This particular line makes a rectangle with the front and back walls and the side wall. The rectangle is constructed both for the forehand and the backhand. The ball obviously has to land within these confines and a high degree of accuracy is required. The main aim of this restriction is to pinpoint the ball which clings to the side wall and also to apply it to strict differences between the varieties of stroke, for example, the drop shot, the drive and the lob.

At its most successful this exercise will force the player to perform with a particularly high level of control because it has the effect of focusing the mind. Tactically, when the player has to confine himself in this way, it has the effect of raising the quality of his play because it eradicates cross-court play which tends to produce an abundance of inaccuracies. It will be noted that all play down the side-wall channel has the protection of the proximity of the wall and poses an immediate problem for the opponent. The closer the side-wall stroke is to the wall, the greater the difficulty for the opponent.

This condition may represent anything but a handicap to the player because of the tactical discipline that it imposes upon him. While the player takes on the straight man, the conditioned game is dictated by the latter because his selection of stroke will force the player to employ the stroke in the rectangle down whichever wall is nearer. For example, any ball right of the centre line will signify a forehand and vice versa. In a situation in which both players are restricted to the side-wall condition, then the specific side wall will be nominated from the start and at a suitable moment the players will change sides. When the two players are operating in the same rectangle, then it is vitally important that they are constantly aware of each other's position because they are in such close proximity that an excessive or sometimes even moderate swing of the racket will be sufficient to cause injury. There is no need whatsoever to take such risks because the rally should be replayed immediately under the rule of let: the penalty point is not used because the emphasis here is on making the strokes, not on refereeing decisions.

Such confines for the players are extremely valuable practices in player movement to and from the ball, in and out of the opponent's path, and are useful when the players return to using the whole court. If the players can overcome the traffic problems in a confined space, then they should be less in one another's way with the whole court at their disposal. This is not the main objective of this conditioned game, but it is a valuable by-product.

Another lesson which may be learned from this is that the player can use good ball control to position his opponent in the court where they do not need to come into physical contact with each other. For example, if the player keeps the ball in front or the back of the court, then he is at liberty to take up position in the middle of the court, merely standing aside as the opponent passes from one to the other.

The cross-court game

This condition is self-explanatory, the line of demarcation being the line on the floor that bisects the mid-court line, extends to the front wall and disappears through the door at the back of the court, assuming that the door is in the middle of the back wall. All the player's strokes should cross this line. Cross-court strokes are generally a source of carelessness and inaccuracy, so it is to this practice that a player will turn to seek the opportunity to improve this aspect of his play.

The important fundamental is that the ball does not finish within easy reach of an opponent who is positioned in the middle of the court. This is the most common failing of any squash player because the ball will then land directly on the opponent's racket with a minimum of movement required. One of the reasons why the Pakistanis are such a high-class squash-playing nation lies in their ability to hit for good width on their cross-court strokes.

The angles game

This exercise requires the player to use the extra wall before the front wall constantly, so playing the angle or the reverse angle off every stroke. This represents a good handicap to the player because of the repeated use of the extra wall, so that the ball takes longer to die and, as a consequence, gives the opponent added time to get to it. It may seem a slightly eccentric exercise, but it does give the player a chance to focus exclusively on the angle strokes and to work out possibilities and uses that he did not see before. In general terms the angle is a badly-used stroke, adopted mainly as a means of returning the ball to the front wall as a last resort; but over the years there have been many top-class players who have used the angle as a severe attacking weapon – players such as Gogi Alauddin, Philip Ayton and Geoff Hunt, the former world champion.

The main objective of this angles game is the exclusive use of the angle to work out the most appropriate options that are available to the player and those which he is most happy to use.

To achieve any success against a straight man in this context, the player will need to employ the angle not only to direct the ball to the front court, but also to experiment with the skid boast to achieve some depth in the back court. The player must not exaggerate the importance of this game, but it does provide much opportunity for experiment and fun as well as the chance to gain some experience. The angles game has an element of fun because it will throw up one or two somewhat comical situations in which the player tries to play the angle off a ball that he would not normally consider. It is important for the player to be able to recognise the element of fun running through all these games because it is a strong motivation for working with dedication and discipline.

All the conditioned games that have been mentioned so far can use the normal scoring system, which is to nine points, the best of five games and points scored for service. But as a variation the player can vary the scoring system to create added interest. Being rigid is of little importance and it is a good challenge to select different numbers upon which to finish the individual game. Equally, the American system of scoring a point for every rally may be used. It hardly needs to be said that is is not necessary to play the best of five all the time, but it is as well to incorporate a deciding game or merely a tie-breaker, for example, the best of three points. For playing conditioned games the purpose is merely to agree the scoring systems in advance so that there is no confusion, and to ensure that the challenge of the competition is engaged.

It is noteworthy that in the squash world there are two scoring systems: the English system and the American system. The essential difference is that the Americans win or lose a point every rally, while in the English system a point can be won only in service. In recent times there have been moves to produce a compromise between the English game of nine points and the American game of fifteen by playing two figures between the two.

It does the player no harm whatsoever to be able to cope with all the different possible scoring systems in the same way as with the discipline of the conditioned game, because he will then become constantly alert and ready to deal with any situation. The overriding aim of these exercises is to make the player alert and mentally prepared for any eventuality.

The conditioned games may be expanded by the further addition of another player or even two, but, as more players are introduced to the court, the emphasis should lie particularly on experimentation with strokes and the fun element along with the competitive instincts should be slightly muted.

The three-ball game

In this exercise three players play individually and the order of play is of prime importance. For example, player A follows B follows C and the *loser* of the rally scores a point and also starts the next rally. As a result, the first player to reach the specified number becomes the loser. There can be a conspiratorial nature to this game, but it is destructive to the overall objective which is that each player should use every opportunity to employ the full range of his strokes, adjust to the movements in and around the extra player and negotiate the timing difference of not playing alternately. This is a game of fun and is especially useful as a warm-up exercise for more pressure-intensive work.

The additional player in this game will provide an extra time-span for each player to prepare and execute each stroke better with more time at his disposal, and he should take the chance to perfect his strokes. The game may become conspiratorial when two players play against one because the first player makes an easy set-up ball for the second player to hit for a winner. The players must take part as individuals. The order of play may be altered and strict insistance on the correct order may result in extra points being awarded for playing out of order. The alternative to A follows B follows C is A follows C follows B.

Doubles

The extra player is added in this routine to make the normal doubles formation and in squash the pairs return the ball alternately. It is more normal for the teams to play forehand side and backhand side as opposed to front court and back court. The front and back formation is particularly dangerous for players who are new to the game because the player at the front frequently becomes a target.

The important safety requirement in doubles is that the players attempt to stay in the middle of the court as much as possible except when they have to move to the corners to return the ball. Wherever else the players may end up, it is prudent to keep away from the side and front walls for safety's sake. The penalty point does not exist in doubles, so that let becomes a device for player safety and if there should be any doubt in a

A doubles match and some eminent players: from the left, Lisa Opie, Alison Cummings, Fiona Greaves and Barbara Diggens. This is played on a singles court and good practitioners can play the game safely without too much risk of getting in each other's way.

player's mind about a possibly dangerous outcome of his impending stroke, then he should stop play immediately.

Doubles then, as in other sports, is a team game and it contains appropriate tactics that provide an added dimension to the singles game. It is this broadening of experience for which doubles is a valuable practice exercise for the singles player. At its simplest doubles can be fun after a lengthy practice session and the value of such relaxation is never to be underestimated.

Doubles is a game for which there is not a surfeit of competitive opportunities, but that does not invalidate the strength of the case for using it as a good practice opportunity. The rules for doubles are based on the American scoring system, for which a point is scored at the conclusion of every rally and a game lasts for fifteen points. The teams divide into one and two for service purposes and server one continues to serve until he loses a rally, at which point server two takes over. When that rally is lost, the service transfers to the opposing team.

As in some of the earlier conditioned games, doubles has a merit in that the player has only half the court to cover – and equally so for the opposition of course. A premium, therefore, is set on greater accuracy of stroke, particularly in search of outright winners, and also tactical awareness. It is, after all, much harder to stroke the ball to an area of the court where there is no opponent, so stroke selection becomes complicated or at best more difficult. The final benefit is that the court is cluttered with players, so the individual player will learn to move around the other players and anticipate such situations better.

One versus two

This is the best practice match of all because it combines the individual pitting his skills against the defensive capabilities of a doubles pairing. It is normally played to a singles scoring system, although this is not essential. The interesting tactical factor is that the player cannot attempt to outlast or beat the pair on purely defensive qualities because they should have sufficient resources between them to wear down the physical reserves of the individual systematically. The individual must go on to the attack and attempt to win rallies by accurate stroke-making and by outmanoeuvring and out-thinking his opponents. The player must put all his faith in his ability with the the racket to play the quality of strokes that will pressurise the pair. This is the only aspect, allied to sound tactical thinking, in which the player has the opportunity to be on level terms. If the pair begin to dominate the player on his own, then they can run him systematically from corner to corner until eventually the player is forced into an error or is out of position. Clearly it is extremely difficult for the player to tempt the pair out of position.

This exercise has the effect of sharpening the blade of the player's attacking game, thereby putting him on his mettle, and is particularly valuable in the final stages of preparing for a major event. It is most effective as a short, sharp exercise because of the intense pressure which it generates, although obviously each of the three participants can take turns against a pairing.

Match practice

The final area of concern in practising is match play itself. There is no substitute for the experience of match play because the player is then coming to terms directly with what will happen to him in his quest for success in the sport. The big difference between match practice and actual match play is the added pressure of the big occasion. Unfortunately it is impossible to cater for this pressure in a practice situation, so the more actual match experience the player can obtain in tournaments and in leagues the better. Match practice is the opportunity to go through all the motions, attempting to play at the highest levels, before going into the pressure situation of the big match.

Throughout his practice matches the player should always be trying new ideas, new strokes and different tactics because in the game situation there is little or no opportunity to be so self-indulgent. The main priority then will be to employ the right tactics to win. There are some players who play much their best squash in practice and are unable to release the same ability on the big occasion because of nerves. On the other hand, there are some players who are hopeless and not motivated in practice and need the kick of the big occasion when there is something at stake to play their best squash.

The player must choose the different types of practice partner at his disposal carefully, and should be clear in his own mind what type of game the ensuing match will provide. For example, if he picks the practice partner who is motivated only on the big occasion, then he may not have much opposition to an easy victory. The player must not be lulled into a false sense of security, so for the purposes of a good match, he may find it necessary to consider staking a small wager on the outcome of such a practice match. Equally, if the player selects a partner who is brilliant in practice, but not so on the big occasion, then he must be careful not to be too depressed if he should suffer a heavy defeat. It may be wise to avoid such a practice except when the player is ready and prepared for the test. The player must also select his practice partner with a view to the type of tactics that they employ, because the tournament and league matches will throw up opposition of different playing characteristics.

In the same way, the player should be well aware of the temperature in which his major matches will be conducted and he should attempt to simulate the same in his pre-match practising. For example, it is not unknown for international players who are to travel to play in Pakistan to select a red or blue-dot ball, which are livelier and bouncier, and also to turn up the heating on the courts when the club owner is not looking! In the club internal leagues players can quite often be seen on cold courts in the middle of winter playing with yellow-dot balls, when it could produce a better match if the players, in conjunction with the league organiser, were to agree to play with a white-dot ball.

The player must be aware of the different match plan and tactics as well as the strength of his opposition and select his practice partners accordingly. For example, it would be pointless for the player to practise with a hard-hitting partner who favours the back-court areas if he is about to face a touch player who is especially adept in the front court, and vice versa. It may not always be possible to practise with an identical copy of a future opponent, but players of similar characteristics are just as valuable.

The most important aspect of match practice is that on a regular basis – for example, once a week or once a fortnight – the player should be able to select a partner who is able to beat him convincingly. This is because it is in rising to such a challenge that the player stands to learn the most and also the quickest. Such a player will frequently be the local coach or the club champion or even the best player in the next league above. The important consideration is that the player selected has a greater skill from which there is much to be learnt. The player must approach such a match with determination and a strong desire to stay on court as long as possible, making himself as difficult to beat as he can. In this way the player can see the tricks at a higher standard at first hand. Just as important for the player is that, in addition to learning this lesson in defeat, he must counter-balance his overall practice plan with somebody whom he can beat in order to restore some of his confidence and equally to help the other player to learn. Ideally, in this manner the atmosphere in any club would be conducive only to improving the overall standards of squash played.

Match practice should form a greater part of the players's diet before the big game, provided that suitable practice partners are available. As many players will have found, if there is a lack of partners and the pre-match diet consists largely of practice exercises, then it will be more difficult to arrive at the match so thoroughly prepared, despite rigorous efforts made in practice and training. However, it has to be admitted that some players are able to cope with just this facility.

Whatever happens in a practice match, the player should always remember that a good win is never as good, nor a bad loss ever so bad, as he might imagine, because they really matter only in the tournament or league-match situation when there is something extra at stake.

The player can now follow through some ideas and routines of a working practice model, which represents a seven-day period of preparation before a tournament. The model is by no means definitive and should be adapted to suit each individual's requirements. This model can be developed to incorporate longer periods of preparation, but fundamentally all the ideas are taken from the preceding chapters. Its importance is derived from the need to work on all the aspects of practice because they would be worth nothing if the player did not look towards a routine which would give him a meaningful opportunity to consider all points of his game constructively to the improvement of the whole.

Obviously every player's needs are governed by his individual strengths and weaknesses, but opposite is an example of a possible working week before an event which is important to the individual at whatever level it may be. The emphasis should be on discipline and commitment to the task; sloppiness will eventually be reflected in a weakness during a match, possibly at nine-nine in the fifth and deciding game when it can least be afforded. Even on days when the player does not relish the practice, the routine must be maintained.

The general pattern is to work out in short, light sessions in the mornings before moving on to the main activity in the afternoons, which will demand high levels of fitness and application. Towards the end of the week there is provision for rest and relaxed practice so that there is still an appetite for the competitive match. Four players are ideal to share the routine because it caters for the maximum variety of activities and at match practice the player can either play one other player to the best of five games or each of the other three to the best of three games. If a group of four players is not available, then the practices must be adapted accordingly. All the skill practices, warm-ups and double feed sessions are to be extracted from the routines already detailed.

There is little recourse to any hard physical training off the court because it is assumed that, so close to a major game, the player will find it more appropriate to concentrate on racket skills. In addition, his physical preparations should have been done in advance of getting ready for the game. There is, however, a provision for warm-ups and periods of warming down at the beginning and end of the day's work. These will become good habits for all future squash activity and should become intensely personal to the requirements of the in-

The working model

		10.30 a.m. – 12.00 noon	2.30 p.m. – 5.00 p.m.
	Day one	½ hour warm-up – stretching – knock up 1-hour skills – angles, lobs, drop shots, volleys	Pressure practice – double feed (single stroke routines) – one *v* two game, warm-down
	Day two	½-hour warm-up 1-hour conditioned games (side-wall cross-court)	Match practice Warm-down
	Day three	½-hour warm-up 1-hour conditioned games (back-court, short)	Pressure practice – 1 hour double feed (combination of strokes) – 1½ hours one *v* two game Warm-down
	Day four	½-hour warm-up 1 hour skills – drop shot, nicks, kills	Match practice Warm-down
	Day five	½-hour warm-up 1 hour skills – nicks, drops, kills, volleys	Match practice Warm-down
	Day six	Warm-up Conditioned games (side-wall, cross-court, back-court, short)	Pressure practice – one *v* two game Warm-down
	Day seven	Warm-up Conditioned games (doubles, three-ball, angles)	Rest

dividual, but the important factor is that such warm-up and warm-down activities are not neglected.

The main object of the week's work is to give the player the chance to be able to play attacking, error-free squash and to use the routine for match-winning purposes. Confidence should result from this, which takes the player half-way towards winning the important matches.

Jahangir Khan with his coveted British Open trophy – the squash equivalent of the Wimbledon men's singles cup

7. Fitness and health

Squash has enjoyed an almost obsessional rapport with fitness and health at a time when there is a general awareness about them in society. There appear to be several areas of specific concern and these often relate to the degree of commitment and the ability to play. But it is important to appreciate that the sport is of such a violent and physically taxing nature that it will expose any unknown physical problems if sufficient respect is not paid to the body before starting to play.

Fitness for squash

There have been frequent accusations in the media that squash is a killer, but these are perhaps more than a little strong. It is true that there has been a succession of heart attacks on the squash court, but it is by no means certain that all of these have been caused as a direct result of playing squash and that such attacks would not have occurred at that particular time in any form of day-to-day life. It is certain, though, that if there is such a weakness, then squash can ruthlessly expose the problem if the player does not show due care and consideration. It is important, then, that if a player is starting out, particularly at a later stage in life, he should take sensible precautions and consult a medical practitioner. Equally, if the player has not led a physically active life, it is advisable for him to ease gently into the game. For example, it is better to begin by merely hitting the ball on a frequent basis.

'Little and often' is the adage for the introduction and in particular the services of an acknowledged coach will help the beginner not to overdo his initial exertions. The recognised coach will be well able to supervise and monitor the progress so that the player will not be allowed to push himself to unknown physical limits. The greatest danger lies in the violent change from inertia to vigorous activity and it is just such a situation that may cause the body to rebel and expose any deficiency. The emphasis for the beginner, then, should always lie in mastering the racket skills – that is, hitting the ball – while at the same time treating the physical activity with respect.

One particular source of discussion has been a report by Dr Robin Northcote, a research fellow at Glasgow's Victoria Infirmary, who analysed individuals aged forty or more who took up vigorous exercise at a time when they were naturally at a greater risk of heart disease or heart failure. Dr Northcote reported in the *British Heart Journal*:

> This study indicates that squash is a physiologically demanding sport which places a severe strain on the myocardium for considerable periods of time and is capable of generating cardiac arrhythmias. These findings are particularly important for an individual already at risk of sudden death from coronary artery disease or structural cardiovascular abnormalities. Medical advice before participation in the game will identify those at high risk of cardiovascular disease. Subjects in this study who developed arrhythmias were not, however, identified by history, examination or exercise electrocardiography. Thus it seems unwise to begin playing squash after the age of forty years. Whether subjects in this age group already participating in the game should continue to play remains a matter of individual judgement.

This is, in effect, a very clear health warning about the dangers in the sport. They have been a popular theme of exaggeration in the media, but must be taken seriously by those concerned. At the same time there are many people of forty and more playing the sport. Some go on into their sixties and seventies, notably the former British Open champion Hashim Khan, who has continued to compete in the British Vintage section for over-55s.

Dr Northcote said that there had been about sixty sudden deaths that were squash-related since 1977, but added: 'That can be put into context for the sport is ever-expanding as a popular participant activity and the fact that the Squash Rackets' Association believe that there are in excess of three million players now indicates that the fatalities are very much a minority. The significant increase of the minority is sadly not completely surprising as the sport expands further.'

There are sensible precautions that can be taken and one warning is for players to avoid what has been termed the 'pride factor'. That concerns those players who would literally die before losing to an opponent. In such an instance the body's safety valve, in which pain becomes a warning of imminent disaster, can be overridden by a player's total commitment to beating an opponent for the sake of pride and then the ultimate price is paid. The theme of the pride factor was taken up in the Squash Rackets' Association's 1984-85 annual by one of their medical consultants, Dr John Williams, who wrote:

> It is better to be beaten by a better or fitter player than to run yourself into your coffin trying to catch up. The S.R.A. must do their best to make their sport foolproof, but they cannot make it bloody foolproof. All sports carry an element of risk: some are more risky than others. This is as true in squash as in any other sport, but provided that players observe the safety code and, where appropriate, have regular medical check-ups, squash should prove no more risky than any other activity and, indeed, should be a source of great pleasure and relaxation. In the last analysis, however, it is up to each individual player to apply commonsense and restraint to his sporting as well as other activities.

One particular category of concern is the businessman who has put on weight because of a healthy business expense account and who used to play a good game of squash. He has let it lapse, but then decides to resurrect the interest, trying to match his strong, youthful competitive instincts from the start. Such a businessman tends to be highly motivated and determined and is not enamoured of the idea of doing anything at less than 100 per cent. This can be a lethal mixture and is not to be recommended. There are other categories of player who do not necessarily come from the same walk of life, but come into the sport in the same physical situation. In all these cases it must be a slow and painstaking task to begin an active squash life.

Dr Northcote concluded: 'Squash places a severe workload on the heart not found in most other sports.' With due respect to that workload, it is important to prepare the heart muscle for such activity by a sensible warm-up period of exercise. Obviously any doubts should be put to the medical experts before this and an examination is never being excessively cautious if there should be any concern. The maxim 'Get fit to play squash rather than play squash to become fit' is a good one because it pays healthy respect to the possible dangers of the sport. In essence, the heart has the most important function of all the muscles in the body because it pumps the blood to the other muscles, providing the fuel or means by which the others can operate efficiently. Any pull or strain on the heart muscle will have a catastrophic effect and it is with this in mind that the player must warm up all the muscles in the body, but particularly the heart.

The heart can be prepared for impending vigorous activity by gently raising the breathing level, by running on the spot, by doing some step-ups on to a bench at a low height, by trying some shadow court movements or by doing some light skipping. This stimulates the heart to an increased workload, preparatory to confronting the heavy requirements of the sport. Most significantly, it prevents the stress of thrusting upon the resting heart a workload built upon the demands of a vigorous squash game with its accompanying sudden burst of activity. It is better at all times to raise the workload level by degrees so that the heart, like any machine, warms up thoroughly to work efficiently at maximum load.

In consideration of the ultimate price that might be paid for physical carelessness, there are also less dramatic by-products of an excessively vigorous introduction to squash activity. The list of injuries such as pulled muscles and strained backs can be seemingly endless, but again these can be avoided by direct reference to the professionals, both medical and coaching. It may seem to be a great inconvenience to have to prepare so painstakingly for what essentially may be only a hobby, but at the same time the rewards are great because of the sport's requirement of both mental and physical commitment. Once the player achieves the routine and forms the habit of playing regularly, squash can have exactly the same kind of addiction as

David Campbell, Marketing Director of Shulton UK. His company sponsors the British Under 23 Closed Championships. Part of his motivation for the sponsorship could be his own enthusiasm for the game!

other sports. It can become a regular requirement for the release of the frustration encountered by the player during his working day and it will also be a healthy by-product of his improved overall life-style.

There is also a convenience factor associated with squash that derives from the sure and explosive burst of activity which ensures that, assuming precautions are taken in conjunction with the health requirements, a degree of fitness can be attained in a very short period of time. This is especially useful for players with long working days who would find it difficult to comit themselves to other more time-consuming fitness activities. At the same time the racket and ball aspects must not be forgotten because they are essential basics that make squash a sport rather than purely a means towards enhancing health.

So far the beginner or the lapsed player have been the areas of concern. But there is another category to consider – those people who play squash to a reasonable proficiency and use its competitive nature purely as a means of keeping fit. These players form a group who are accustomed to taking part in regular matches and play frequently with the same partners week in and week out. They are often not concerned about enhancing their racket skills, but prefer merely to play regularly in five-set matches, wherever possible, with the main aim being 'to have a good sweat'. These players do not normally indulge in specific pre-match preparations of a fitness or physical nature. On the other hand they tend to play with a frequency that maintains steady levels of physical condition and it is to this habit-forming routine that beginners should aspire as a basis for physical well-being. It is noticable that such regulars tend not to have great problems with their health. Perhaps they will suffer from the occasional niggle or strain, but by and large they are not forever requiring medical assistance. These players do not include in their ranks the unfortunate person who has a genuine accident nor the perennial hypochondriac whose bag will contain more medical provisions than squash equipment!

Warm-up exercises

There is much that can be done to help the muscles of the body other than the heart. They also need the same acceleration of activity as part of the preparation for playing. To warm up the remaining muscles that are used in the game, only smooth and easy movements are required, using just the body weight. There are no prizes for stretching to the limit at the outset because that

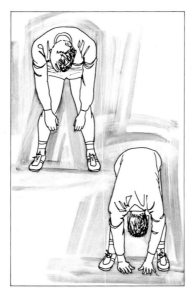

is likely to lead to injury and the aim is to try to avoid the risks and the niggling setbacks that can hamper a player. Instead, he is expected to stretch gradually to the full mobility range.

There are a number of routines that are valuable as warm-up exercises:

1   The player stands upright with his feet apart and gradually bends forward so that his arms eventually touch the floor between his feet. If at first the player does not reach the floor, then he should not force it and the movement should be smooth and easy until he is finally able to do so.

2   In the same upright position the player leans with his arm at his side, extending the hand towards the side of the kneecap. This is repeated, alternating between the right and left side lead. It is again important not to seek the final position at once, but to work gradually towards it.

3   Again in the same upright position, the player raises both arms to shoulder level and rotates his trunk from the waist, keeping his backbone straight, so that he is twisting the lower back and shoulders gently. This is repeated by pivoting to the right and left sides.

4   In the same standing position the player balances on one leg and raises his other knee to his chest, slowly returning it. He then alternates each knee.

5   In a sitting position on the bench in the changing room the player outstretches one leg, pointing the toe and rotating the

foot so that it is circling about the ankle. The legs should again be alternated, as should the circling movement in both clockwise and anti-clockwise directions.

6 Just before the player finishes his warm-up routine, it is helpful just to practise both the forehand and the backhand footwork positions with right leg leading for the backhand and the left leg leading for the forehand. The player may use this as a means of loosening the muscles by actually stretching further than would be necessary in a match. It also has the effect of attuning the player to the forthcoming movements which will be required of him. In this exercise he should alternate between the backhand and forehand.

The key factor, as has already been suggested, is that the player starts off all these exercises quite gingerly and gradually before working to his full capacity. It is foolhardy to rush such a process because the only loser will be the player, who may then suffer the injury that he has been trying to avoid.

These are simple exercises, which need not occupy a long time, but they do prepare a player for more intense physical activity. After these exercises have been completed, it is necessary to raise the breathing level and, as a result, the heart rate, so that the player is thoroughly prepared for the start of the knock-up which precedes a competitive game.

There are many exercises which a player can use to prepare for a match, but the simplest are perhaps the most effective and it is important never to neglect a warm-up, so it guards against neglect if he memorises the routines and ensures that they are easy to employ. The player should never be afraid to use any exercises of his own if they should be particularly suitable or of specific help to the individual.

Diet

There is another area which it is imperative that the player should consider carefully with regard to his health and fitness, and that is his eating and drinking habits. He should always be aware of their importance in helping him to attain his maximum physical potential, especially in the final moments of his build-up to a match.

The player should not forget that his diet is an integral part of his health and fitness in the same way as petrol is vital to the smooth running of a car. There is no need for undue concern because it is normally sufficient to eat sensibly and regularly at appointed times. It is in the player's best interests to maintain a balanced diet, but regularity is the key. In contrast, it is unwise to miss meals or to eat only chocolate without the other foods that make up the total diet.

Frequently the topic of alcohol is raised. The consensus of medical opinion is that it may be beneficial rather than detrimental to the player's game, but again the watchwords are in moderation and at sensible times, for example, never just before a match. Players at the highest levels sometimes abstain totally and this is because it is part and parcel of their personal and psychological discipline rather than for any particular dietary concern.

Finally, the player should be advised to time his major meals after his matches. It is foolhardy to attempt to digest a heavy meal an hour or two before an important match. It is far more advisable for the player to take a light snack of easily digestible food in the hours preceding the match.

If the player should have any doubts about his diet, then it is no problem for him to take medical advice, particularly if he is run-down or suffering from anaemia. A doctor can quite often recommend foodstuffs which, allied to the rest of his health care, should rectify the problem. It is good for a player to eat healthily and well in exactly the same way as a car will normally run much better on high-grade fuel.

The fact that squash players fall into different categories means that they all have varying physical demands made on them. They take up the activity for a variety of reasons, which may not be very dissimilar, but still have an effect on the health and fitness area concerned, so it is necessary to look at these groups with an eye to their respective needs and characteristics.

Juniors

The question is frequently asked: 'At what age should a child start to play squash?' It is never easy to produce a definitive answer, but the possibility has been explored by one eminent coach on his two-year-old son, who merely dragged a full-size racket around the court and tried to put the ball into his mouth! It does seem to be foolish – though not out of the question – to employ a shortened racket for junior players or children, and it is more relevant to give a child the feel of a full-size racket. After all, it is not essential at this stage that the child should hit the ball accurately, but more preferably cleanly.

There is no doubt that children are fast learners and it is necessary for a future champion to make an early start on learning the game. To this end there are currently junior tournaments starting at under-10 level. Parental influence should be brought to bear to ensure that the commitment to junior tournaments is in moderation; and the child should not be forced to put up with

The future of squash rests with its junior players. Seen here at the British Under 10/12/14 winners presentation are former England Internationals Bob Johnson (now with sponsoring company) and Paul Millman representing the Squash Rackets Association. Such encouragement is vital to the life blood of the game

excessively rigorous squash and fitness training programmes. Obviously there are also educational needs which will mitigate against such an early and heavy commitment to the sport. But this is not to underplay the demands of a child whose enthusiasm for the sport is rich, but merely a reminder that any squash routines should be harnessed to the total development of the child. It can also be disturbing for a child to find himself pressurised for successes at a time of life when his physical development may not be as advanced as that of his peers. This might have a discouraging effect and kill much of the initial keenness. The physical disadvantages of a child in terms of size and youthful development are such that the emphasis must be on learning to play the sport while at the same time trying to derive full enjoyment from it.

The role of fitness in junior squash tends to be replaced by the boundless energy of youth. It never goes amiss to create the good habit of fitness exercises, but it is preferable to demonstrate what they are rather than to stress the overall aim of increasing strength. It is far better to let nature take its course in terms of strength and development towards maturity.

Women squash players

This is a considerably under-subscribed area, probably because the majority are put off by the few who are highly competitive and play to win. But there is no less merit in women's social, leisure and health reasons for taking up the sport and in many clubs the atmosphere is greatly improved by an active female membership. In the present climate of concern for fitness and health, it seems entirely appropriate for squash to form part of a weekly routine, particularly when some female participants are able to help utilise club facilities to the full by playing during off-peak hours in the day.

In the age-old dispute about competitive levels, the prowess of women relative to men is always of interest. There are several aspects to consider in matching the two. First, it is arguable as to whether sheer strength is a deciding factor in its own right because it is the combination of strength and accuracy that culminate in a winning formula, so it has to be said that there is probably not a great deal of difference in this area alone. Second, however, there are what are perhaps the deciding factors of speed off the mark, speed around the court and, most significant of all, the ability to turn quickly. This is where the physiological advantage tends to lie with the men. Finally, there is the question of stamina, but this is rarely put to the test because the differentials of speed and agility are usually sufficient to make the difference.

Women are certainly becoming more competitive and are rightly infiltrating into the men's leagues, which means that to a certain degree they are able to outplay men up to certain standards provided that they have a good basic grasp of technique. In the final analysis it is unlikely that women could ever compete on equal terms at the highest levels, but there is still a vital role for them to play in squash and it should not be deemed either sexist or disparaging that the masculine terminology has been used for the sake of convenience in the descriptive passages in this book.

Businessmen

Members of this group often have a good sporting past and are merely seeking to maintain a healthy sporting life-style in their working worlds of business and entertainment. This is indeed a fine philosophy, but it has inherent drawbacks physically. The problem stems from the likelihood that any of a businessman's sporting successes in the past may become a cause for too much commitment to successes in the present when he is not in such good physical condition as before. Ultimately his pride will not permit him to lose without a fight to the bitter end; this potential health hazard has been covered earlier in this chapter. Suffice it to say at this juncture that the businessman should be using the sport as a means of relaxation and a chance for a light, health-conscious lunch. In fact, there is a considerable convenience factor involved in squash as a sport for the business man whose time is valuable, but who still looks for physical activity to provide a contrast with his predominantly sedentary life-style.

The handicapped

This category is best exemplified by the legendary Leeds player Frank Dobby, who perhaps typifies the spirit of the sport and its physical implications more readily than anybody else. Frank lost a leg at the knee in an accident several years ago, but, with the aid of an artificial replacement, he has fought back to play the sport to the extent that he is now a feared competitor. He is well capable of winning the first game against many players who underestimate his capabilities. It goes without saying that Frank has had to rely on considerable racket skills to overcome his problems of mobility, but an opponent who plays a poor drop shot had better beware because he is not slow to despatch it. In addition, his attitude to the sport can probably best be summed up by saying that he is the only player who can break his leg and return to match play within a couple of days or so on receiving a replacement!

Bearing in mind that the discussion so far has considered the player who is ostensibly fit and well, such an example is a source of encouragement to everybody. It shows quite simply that there is no earthly reason why anybody with the right determination cannot take up the sport and strive to derive maximum enjoyment from it.

Full-time players

Once a player has decided to become a full-time competitor, he will be expected to maintain a life-style which will out of necessity conform to the requirements of a professional calling in sport. It has to be stressed that it is hazardous for any player not to take heed of the basic requirements for fitness and health in squash, but the full-time player owes it to himself and to his chosen vocation to adhere to the highest standards. If this is not the case, then he is likely to restrict his opportunities and his progress quite severely. He has on his side the fact that by the time he decides to take the plunge into full-time working in the sport, he will have already reached considerable heights of fitness in order to be in a position to make the transition at all. Such a player's prime need is to retain his fitness routines so that they become second nature to him because training of a physical character will need to be part and parcel of his way of life.

The physical attributes of a good squash player all require constant work so as to enable him to keep in shape for the rigours and stresses of hard match play. Some players are naturally gifted in this respect, but that does not alter the fact that all these assets can be improved. There are specific areas that need highlighting, but in the final analysis they all form part of the total necessities for a squash player. The fact that these areas are all-consuming increases the fascination of the sport. They consist of stamina, agility, speed and strength, and it is the combination of all these qualities that makes squash so intriguing. For example, combining stamina and speed at first seems to be a contradiction, but inevitably the player will be stronger in one area than the other. It is necessary for him to play more to the stronger quality rather than the weaker and this merely accentuates the attraction of the sport.

Stamina

This is the cardiovascular concept, which can be best served by long-distance running or swimming. The most important aspect to bear in mind is that this type of work can make the player slow and ponderous in his movement around the court, so it is a good idea for him to ensure that this work does not fall too close to a crucial period of matches. Such work forms a good, pre-season base on which he can build his agility, speed and racket skills, but at the same time it does not remove the need for the occasional reminder during a lull in the squash season.

Swimming has particular merit in that it gives cardiovascular work without the pounding on the back, knee and ankle joints which occurs on court and also during long-distance running. In addition, it has a recuperative effect on muscles that are tired, stiff and painful in the aftermath of a long, hard five-game match. There is, however, a drawback in the swimming pool and that is when the squash player is not good enough to cope with cardiovascular work in swimming the distance. Running is measured by longer distances in the pre-season sessions, which are tempered to a mere mile or two during the season. This is all part of the platform of confidence that the player requires, knowing that when patience is a prime virtue, then the stamina is ready and waiting.

Agility

This is not an easy area to highlight because it concerns the quirky nature of the movements that a squash player is required to make. These movement patterns will be explored more fully in the following section on speed, but one particularly significant movement sends the player forward to a certain point and then requires him to return to the middle of the court whenever possible. Often the return will be made with a sideways or backward movement, almost crab-like, and it is this movement pattern that requires a degree of agility and poise to achieve the capacity to play good strokes as the end-product. As those who have tried it will know, running sideways or backwards is not as easy as it may appear, particularly in view of the added difficulty of a player concentrating on the next stroke in the rally. The more efficiently that the player copes with this movement, the greater will be his scope for good performance. Another aspect of agility is being able to turn quickly when the player has been wrong-footed, and it is in this area that women have less facility than men in general terms because of their physiological make-up.

Glen Brumby, the World-ranked Australian who is based in Germany, demonstrates his own suppling exercises

Agility has its roots in the suppleness of the body, the capacity for muscles to stretch efficiently, and good mobility in the joints to give the player the ability to perform the movements with more efficiency. Such flexibility will also be of value to the player in avoiding injury and part of this section on agility is already relevant in the warm-up. Above all, the greater the player's suppleness, the better equipped he is in all departments of the sport.

Agility is also particularly relevant when the player is under pressure and is making a final stretch or lunge to retrieve the ball. One notable player, Ali Aziz, the Egyptian who was once ranked among the world's top ten, was quite capable of doing the splits in the final stride when pressed to return the ball. Such a capacity requires the suppleness of an Olympic gymnast, not only to take up the position in the first instance, but also to be able to return to the mid-court area. This movement is difficult enough in normal circumstances, but is considerably more awkward from the splits position.

This aspect of agility is still a relatively unexplored area, specifically in respect of squash, but the general principles of mobility and flexibility are pertinent. The all-round facility provided by an Olympic gymnast's knowledge is broadly the base, but the squash player must have a specific direction to the parts of the body which require most attention for his sport. Such attention will be focused on the legs, hips and back areas, while mobility in the shoulder will be achieved by long hours of stroke-play work. The player must concern himself with the full stretching potential of the muscles and joint mobility in these areas of legs, hips and back. He must gently work towards a greater degree of suppleness in such movement by using merely his own body weight to prepare agility to enhance his squash movements.

Speed

The sooner that the player can reach his ball for the stroke, then the greater the variety of stroke selection will be, either early, late or at the top of the bounce as normal. The later that the player arrives at the ball, then the fewer options there will be and the more predictable his next stroke will be, giving an advantage to his opponent. The major requirement is for speed off the mark, so such training as interval or shuttle running or any method by which the player has to sprint in short, sharp bursts of five, ten or fifteen-yard distances will be valuable. A further alternative is to develop the sprint shuttles in accordance with

Hashim Khan still plays tournament squash well into his sixties. Perhaps the knees don't bend as much as they used to do, but there is no shortage of skill and experience and – most importantly – enjoyment

the court movements, running to its four corners as well as the two points at the side walls where the mid-court lines join the wall. This offers six targets for sprinting and returning to the middle of the court, usually playing a shadow stroke on arrival at each destination. This exercise is often timed to see if the player can increase his number per minute, so testing his improving speed or otherwise. This routine does have a drawback, though, in that the player may rush excessively, leaving himself unable to balance to play the stroke in the quest for improvement.

It is often advisable also to do the speed work away from the confines of the court so that the quirky squash movements are not bastardised by too much haste. It should always be remembered that in the end the player's main need is to strike the ball cleanly and accurately, so there is no place for rushing as many strokes as possible because that tends to hand the advantage to the opponent if they are not under control.

Speed is often a natural gift because it is a quality with which some players appear to be well endowed. In contrast others are not so swift and they have to compensate by working hard to make the movement as efficient as possible. This applies in particular to those players who are not of a sprinter's stature, but who are tall and gangling or of a clumsy disposition or otherwise less fortunate. Raw speed has been a priority in this context, but it must always be assessed in relation to balance and agility.

Strength

This provides resilience and allows the player to play at full potential or as close to it as possible for the duration of the match. Leg strength has been partially considered under the headings of stamina and speed, but there is a general conditioning of the remaining parts of the body which will give the player confidence in the longevity and power of his performance provided that the necessary upper-body strength is available. In the same way that leg strength is a blend of speed and stamina, upper-body strength is the combination of power and agility.

There are two fundamental ways in which a player can work on body strength. The first and most obvious is by the use of weight-training facilities and the second is by working on a circuit-training series of exercises that utilise the player's own body strength. For the sake of variety the player can combine the two. In the first instance the player can be best served by consulting a weight-training expert, but in the forefront of his mind

Press-ups

Squat thrusts

Sit-ups

Leg raises

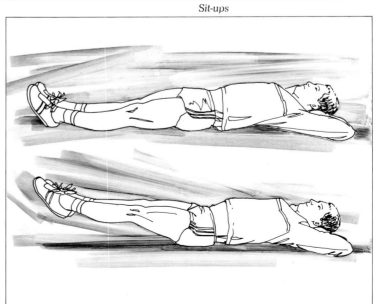

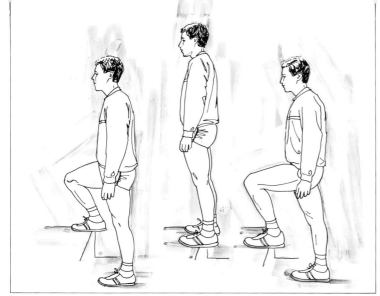

Step-ups

Star jumps

Double knee jumps

will be the knowledge that the needs of squash are better suited to light weights and repetitions, recognising the necessity for speed of movement in the sport. In the same way that long-distance running can make the player ponderous, so heavy weights can make the player strong without the necessary speed for racket movement. Circuit-training, on the other hand, is more reminiscent of the original physical education class at school, but there are some useful exercises that can be put together to form a session that will help squash. These are:

1   *Press-ups.* The player takes up the normal press-up position, facing the floor while balancing on the hands and toes. By lowering the body to the floor without actually touching it and returning to the original position, the arm strength will be improved.

2   *Squat thrusts.* The player again starts from the press-up position with the body supported by the arms and balanced on the toes. From this position the legs are brought up so that the feet are as far forward as possible and then returned to the press-up position.

3   *Sit-ups.* With his hands behind his head, the player raises the body from the lying to the sitting position and back again. The legs should remain flat on the floor throughout. As a safeguard for the player it is better to do this exercise with the legs bent at the knees, however, because such movement with the legs flat on the floor can cause back problems.

4   *Leg raises.* The player is again flat on his back with his hands behind his head. Keeping his legs straight, he gently raises both legs together approximately twelve inches from the floor, pauses and then lowers them again.

5   *Step-ups*. These require a bench or something similar on to which the player will step and stand to his full height before returning to stand on the floor again. This exercise leads with the same foot, but the leading foot should be changed after the repetition.

6   *Star jumps*. From a standing position, the player jumps to lift his body off the ground and at the same time spreads his arms and legs to form a star shape. He then returns to the ground with his arms and legs as they originally were.

7   *Double knee jumps*. This is a similar exercise to star jumps except that from his standing position the player jumps to clasp his knees to his chest with his arms in a tucked position before releasing the relevant parts of the body to land as he originally was.

All these exercises are done to repetitions. At the outset they can be timed to give the repetition numbers, but alternatively set targets of repetitions can be given. It is quite normal for a player to work through a circuit of this kind several times. As he starts to cope with it more efficiently, the repetitions will obviously be increased as he strives constantly to improve his performance.

The strictly physical aspect is an integral part of a squash player's working life, but it should always be balanced carefully with the more important attention to racket skills. It is fair to say that with good training the body can be made to work more efficiently, but there is infinite scope for a player to improve his racket skills and his court craft. It is with this in mind that a three to four-hour working day on the court, the player must allocate about half-an-hour to an hour for off-court work in addition. This then reflects the balance between the two areas. At the same time it should be remembered that this is by no means applicable to all players. It is intended as a useful guideline, but some individuals will no doubt have their own interpretations.

It is of the utmost importance, however, that all players take into account the health and fitness factors. They cannot be considered too lightly because so much depends on them, whatever level a player may have reached. They are essential for both safety and more aesthetic reasons. Above all, squash cannot exist satisfactorily if its participants do not recognise or understand their full importance.

8. The coach

Throughout the length and breadth of the squash world, clubs are divided into the 'haves' and the 'have-nots' as far as possessing a coach is concerned. By and large such provisions are haphazard, but it is in the hands of the coaches that the future of the game lies, so all aspects of the coach and his role must be considered in detail.

Many types of coach willingly offer their services, at different cost levels. The Squash Rackets' Association has well-defined coaching courses and examinations for the enthusiast, and this operation is spearheaded by the national coach. Over the years the job of the national coach has changed, but it was perhaps at its most productive at the outset when it was in the capable hands of first Tony Swift, a notable player in his own right, and later Peter Hartley. After the initial labours in the coaching field, however, the job became more administrative and organisational, but this is the official channel from which the players and coaches of tomorrow are created.

There are also many coaches who are not products of this official approach. They vary from top players of proven playing capability to the teacher who has little experience, but enjoys a sociable session on the court. Unfortunately, it is from this latter type that coaches in general may be liable to acquire a bad reputation. That is not to say that these 'part-timers' do not make good coaches, but inevitably there will be some bad eggs in the basket, so it is important that the learner selecting his coach makes sure he is training with somebody capable of doing a good job. There is nothing more damaging than going to a coach who is merely interested in making a living and does not fully appreciate the requirements of an aspiring player. At the same time, there are coaches of proven quality who have not emerged through the normal channels. In the minefield of good and bad coaches, it is not easy to find the right way, but it is always valuable to take advice from any past pupils or even from the S.R.A. themselves or anyone whose advice is likely to be good. The final selection always lies with the player himself and from the day that the beginner picks up a racket to the day that he reaches accomplishment and beyond, it will never be easy to seek out a coach who is precisely suited to his own needs. It is never an easy decision, and at the end of the day a choice of coach is often highly individual because there are some coaches and their pupils who are inseparable and by the same token there are players who would never be able to cope with certain coaches.

There are some players who even now believe that they have little need of a coach, and this is merely an attitude of mind. The right coach will be able to develop the game of any pupil to a new level provided that the pupil is prepared to make a commitment. This is a fact at whatever level of participation and involvement the player has. The fact that some players should feel that they have no need of a coach is a reflection of either a low level of commitment to the game or a bad experience from past coaches. Such an attitude is detrimental to the overall development of the game.

The coach then has a role to play throughout a player's career, but it is one that changes and develops through the various stages.

The coach and the beginner

This is the biggest market as far as the coach is concerned and it is at this stage that the coach needs the greatest powers of patience and perseverance. Loosely, this is the formative stage when the coach teaches the beginner the basic strokes and takes him to the point of being able to play the game and having a knowledge of the rules.

At its simplest squash is a game in which a ball is struck against a wall, and that in itself can provide a player with much pleasure. But from the outset the coach is trying to provide the newcomer with a direction that will be more challenging in the middle and long-term and therefore more interesting still. In the great squash boom of recent years, which has probably tapered off to some extent now, there was possibly a shortage of coaches, so all the newcomers were self-taught. However, this left the newcomers open to the 'novelty value' syndrome because they did not have the impetus that a coach can provide. Their dalliance with the sport was therefore shorter-lived than it should have been.

It is crucial that the coach overcomes the initial novelty value that players derive from simply hitting the ball against the wall with the racket, and set the newcomer's course for a longer-term acceptance of the greater challenges and enjoyments that the sport has to offer. The coach's role is so important because he is not only responsible for introducing the player to the sport, but also for maintaining the player's interest in it. The coach's job and his success at it will reflect his own enthusiasm, enjoyment and devotion to the sport and he will often influence the player as much by his personality as by what he has to teach. So the coach has a great responsibility, especially with beginners, to teach the sport correctly and also to convey a healthy and enjoyable attitude to it.

The coach and the club player

The author, team captain of Leeds club Armley in the American Express National League, seen here advising the up and coming team member Bryan Beeson

By this stage, it is assumed that the player can play the game and that the coach's main preoccupation will be with improving the quality of his play. This is a more extensive and organisational role, since it should not take coach a long time to help a beginner to play the game. However, the development of higher standards of play is a long-term objective and the coach's role will develop accordingly to the point when – and if – the player is good enough, or wishes to play the game as a full-time committed player who seeks to earn his living from it. The coach must

create an organised package for the player which, among other things, must fit in with his job and general life-style so that the player is able to work consistently for the higher challenges in his game.

For instance, the player will no doubt start his playing career at the bottom of the club's internal leagues. But with good work and coaching the player should ideally progress through these leagues to a point where he is capable of representing the club's teams in the local or regional leagues, and so on to the county side and beyond. Throughout the period of time that such progress will take, the coach will look for regular sessions with the player, maybe weekly, so that he can monitor the developments of his game, organise the strengths, improve on the weaknesses and give tactical advice. The coach will require his pupil to practice and to endure the pressure exercises which will prepare him for matches.

This area of work can be particularly stimulating for the coach because the improvements can often be dramatic and the rewards considerable. The organisational aspect of the coach's job is not just in terms of lessons given, but should always include the direction in which the player should progress, always bearing in mind his individual needs. At this stage the coach has assumed an all-embracing coaching responsibility, for it will be insufficient merely to give the player his practice sessions; he will also be required to attend matches for the purposes of analysing the progress that has been made. Further, the assistance that the player will derive from the coach's encouragement must not be forgotten. In this particular role analysis, no player should be omitted from the coach's concern and all the players who attend his lessons at whatever level merit his attention in this manner. If anybody ever thought coaching an easy job, then it has to be said that it is a time-consuming responsibility, but there can also be a strong sense of job satisfaction.

The coach and the full-time player

This is a highly specialised area and requires the detailed knowledge of somebody who has had a long and valuable experience in the playing side of the game. In the previous two categories the coach need not necessarily be experienced at the highest playing levels of the game, and sometimes it can be quite desirable if he is not; but in this category the coach does need that expertise. If it is not inherent in him, then he must organise the availability of such expertise.

The coach must be a capable feeder for the player to be able to practise, and this demands that his ball skills should be of the highest order. Before dealing with this standard of play, the coach will no doubt have been able to compete on equal terms or better with his pupils. At this stage, however, the coach will barely be able to compete with a full-time player except that he does have the advantage of a handicap system.

Apart from the role of a feeder in a practice situation, the coach's job is also one of counsellor. His deep knowledge of the player, not only on court but off it, becomes an intrinsic part of his role. That role is now much less a track-suited one than it was with the beginner or the club player and there is a great deal more pressure because of the fact that the player now needs to win in order to earn a living. This can cause the coach as many problems as, if not more than, the player who uses the sport as a means of relaxation. Being coach to a full-time player is really a full-time job in itself. However, there are few players who can afford such a luxury, so a coach will predominantly fill the roles required by the beginner and the club player; if he is lucky, he may also have the option of working with a full-time player occasionally. There is as much squash coaching experience to be gained from working at the beginning as at the end of the playing scale, and it is the ability to be able to work freely across

Jahangir Khan and his coach Rahmat Khan at the 1985 British Open at Wembley. This is one of the most outstanding player/coach relationships of recent times

the spectrum that gives the coach the greatest possible expertise in fulfilling all his roles.

The coach's part has been considered in relation to some general categories of player who would seek his advice. The coach is generally likely to be retained by the club and to work within its required schedules, but there are some freelance coaches as well. They offer their services on a casual basis, but no less seriously, for a day or more per week in a club and in several different clubs during the course of that week. The most obvious exception is the national coach, who is retained by the S.R.A.

It is now appropriate to look at some of the qualities that a coach will require to fulfil the somewhat ubiquitous activities to be met in the club situation. The coach in squash will not be able to support himself from specific areas, as can the full-time player or the team coach, so he will need to be a so-called jack-of-all-trades, and desirably a master of as many of them as possible. The coach will need working knowledge or even specialist understanding of as many areas as possible to be a top coach. Unfortunately such a talented person is not to be found in great abundance in the sport because essentially he is ambitious and will seek greater fruits from his labours by diversifying into other fields.

A useful comparison may be made between tennis and squash in this respect. In tennis the world's top players have permanent coaching assistance which they hire. In squash, on the other hand, few top players, with the exception of the world champion, Jahangir Khan, have constant coaching back-up. This reflects on the game and is perhaps holding back its fullest development. Nevertheless there are specific assets that a coach should have and these are well worth considering.

Teaching ability

This hardly needs stating, but it is important that good techniques are communicated clearly and in an uncomplicated manner to the pupil. In some cases it is noticeable that there are players who have no clear idea of what they should be trying to achieve. This stems from confused teaching and may be traced to poor coaching, usually by somebody who is not qualified to coach. The coach must have a good grasp of all the requirements of the sport to be able to communicate his knowledge. Part and parcel of good coaching is the coach's own personality, which will have a significant influence upon the attitude of the player.

Ability to motivate

Many players are highly motivated before they reach the coach, but it is the coach's ability to motivate his pupil further that will extend the player to new levels of improvement. It must not be forgotten that there will be times in every player's squash career when he loses form, becomes depressed, and needs a helping hand from a coach to rekindle his enthusiasm. It is particularly difficult sometimes for a player who has suffered what he considers to be a bad defeat against an opponent he feels he should have beaten to raise any enthusiasm for another match. It is then that the coach must grasp the situation, perhaps bearing in mind the axiom that the player is never quite as good as his last victory and never quite as bad as his last defeat. Such level-headed thinking will motivate the player to take up the new challenge in the next match. As far as the coach is concerned, his motivation of players can be an especially difficult task because each one will have his individual characteristics, which means that he will respond to different stimuli. The coach must identify those characteristics and adopt appropriate stimuli.

Analysis

The coach must have a thorough understanding of squash; the specialised knowledge required in his assessment of player's strengths and weaknesses will depend upon the standards of his players. The coach must be able to spot the different abilities of his own players and not only work to improve all these aspects week by week, but also, in watching the course of one specific match, be able to adapt them tactically to produce the goods in that same encounter. He must be able to read the progress of any match, work out what is happening and then convert that knowledge into short and simple hints to the player in his coaching aid between games. This is never easy because the player is under the pressure of the match, in control of his destiny, and he may not even hear or agree with what the coach is saying. There have been occasions when one simple piece of advice, such as: 'Attack the backhand volley high', has had a dramatic effect on a match. Matches can be won or lost on such advice and it is up to the coach to try to find the right advice for a positive result and avoid any negative consequences.

There are times when kind words and a pleasant smile are sufficient, but the responsibility lies with the coach, who has to sort out the safest path through this minefield. The thoroughly organised coach will also be able to size up the opposition and give advice on a match plan to overcome an opponent. This discussion can be very helpful to the player in the pre-match build-up and can be a steadying influence at a time when the player may be racked with nerves and anxiety. It is again the coach's responsibility to handle the situation with the greatest sensitivity and furthermore to make it clear to his charge that if the original match plan should go astray, then he should be flexible enough to adapt and use different tactics.

Quite obviously this is an extremely important area and becomes increasingly so as the player reaches higher standards. It is of particular importance to players at the highest level, but its relevance can hardly be underestimated to the player who is just starting out in the game. The crucial factor is the development of a significant rapport between coach and player; this will be entirely founded upon the coach's expertise and the pupil's trust.

The calming influence

The player has to cope with so much pressure that the presence of a coach who can keep him calm and relaxed will prepare him better to give of his best in crisis situations, like Geoff Hunt, the former world champion from Australia, who was always a calm, unruffled player outwardly. The coach can go a long way towards helping the player to achieve such presence of mind and can particularly help the volatile player to try to channel his energies towards playing rather than outside distractions.

Discipline

There is no doubt that this quality is a vital ingredient for any player searching for success in the sport, and for the beginner it is a quality that can be instilled by the coach from Day One by the tone set in his teaching. This represents the difference between quality and quantity work, and it is the former which the coach should demand from his pupil.

This ingredient pervades the whole of the player's daily life and is noticeable not only in the amount of balls that he strikes into the tin, but also in such circumstances as arriving early or late for the match, with or without all the correct equipment. It is a reflection of the player's total commitment or otherwise to the sport, and a good coach never tires of seeking the highest standards – where practicable – from his pupils. It is required of the coach that his standards of discipline are as high as, if not higher than, those of his players so that he can command this respect and also be able to enforce it.

On a more practical note, there are other obvious assets that a coach should have. He must, for example, be able not only to give helpful tips in individual lessons to a pupil, but also to sort out a programme of practice, training and competitive events so that the player has a complete framework in which to advance his interest and his standard in the sport. This is an area which is sometimes forgotten and has a direct relevance to a player's long-term enjoyment and involvement in squash. The coach must identify the player's requirements and feed them directly, with particular relevance to any possible career commitments, so that a squash diet fits conveniently into his life-style. This not only provides the player with the opportunity to play the game, but also, by recommendation, should encourage the player to watch others of the highest calibre available. It should never be forgotten that one of the best ways to learn is by watching the best players and how they cope with their problems. The coach will further set a good example by being an active playing participant himself at whatever standard he is able to compete. This demonstrates great enthusiasm to aspiring players.

It must be said that the coach's own playing standard is not of vital importance to him because it will be his overall commitment to playing form from which his pupils will learn. Furthermore, it is noteworthy that the best players do not necessarily make the best coaches nor do the best coaches necessarily make the best players. Every coach and player should be judged entirely on his merits by his ability in those areas, but it does not mean that there cannot be useful give and take.

The coach will often be required to be a general dogsbody and factotum to players at the highest levels for all their arrangements of one sort or another. This is because the player at international level will have his hands more than full with trying to play successfully, and it is customary for his coach and/or his manager to remove as many distractions as possible so that he can concentrate solely on playing.

There are two clear areas with which the coach in squash terms will be required to be conversant, simply because of the logistics of tournament playing. They are sponsorship and publicity – and the two are interlinked. It may seem out of the jurisdiction of the coach's brief, but such is the early stage of development in squash that if the coach should recommend a programme of events and the pupil should decide to take them up, then there will inevitably be travelling involved and occasionally accommodation and subsistence to find. So even at a very early stage in a player's career development, such activity needs funding, and not everybody can afford such a commitment. The coach is then faced with two possible solutions. He can amend the original programme of events to avoid extra costs and possibly risk the player missing out on his best opportunity; or the player can assist in trying to raise some sponsorship. Any raising of sponsorship moneys will require the relevant recognition, and this is normally achieved through the Press, whether it be in a club newsletter or in the local newspaper. At the highest levels professional players will have managers or agents to help them in this respect, but at more basic levels it is in the interests of the coach to know as much as he can about all the possibilities that can contribute towards helping his players to reap the best rewards.

It can be seen that the coach's role covers many facets, and this is because there is not a vast amount of wealth in squash at present. The sport is at an early stage of development and there is a great call for many coaches, but this work is vocational rather than lucrative. This perhaps does not currently afford the game the opportunity of having the best qualfied coaches. The majority of coaches fulfil commitments attached to one club, and it is the role of the coach in a club situation to which attention will now be turned. It is here that the coach will bring his assets to bear.

The club coach

The most common role for the club coach is that of individual tuition, either by appointment or at appointed times. This is usually predetermined by the club and the coach at the initiation of their liaison. This is the most obvious role to be fulfilled by the coach in the club, but, in addition to this, he should instigate group or team coaching sessions in which he will be able to work with players of similar standards and characteristics. This provides him with the maximum facility to have players motivating each other, in addition to his own input. The players' individual competitive instincts will enable them to bring the best out of each other, and this also offers the coach the chance to run double-feed and other such sessions which require more than two people on court. It will also allow him to inject as much variety as possible into his sessions in addition to the one-to-one coaching situation. Such group work is always beneficial for the club morale and atmosphere, which, if the group forms the basis of the club team, can continue into the league match situation and hopefully instil more confidence to improve the possibility of team successes.

It is rather expected that the coach will also be involved in playing in teams at some level, which will obviously be determined by his standard. This involvement is important because if not only gives the coach the chance to lead by example, but also to monitor the progress of his pupils and the teams in which they play. The coach will have the overall responsibility of lifting the standing of the club in the local leagues and frequently he will be judged by its playing standard vis-à-vis the others in the area, as well as by the amount of work which he puts into his coaching.

More often than not the club who has a history of involvement in competition will find this the most rewarding aspect of his work. However, in being the administrator of this playing activity, he may well find himself with the additional problems of securing sponsorship and publicity. He may not be directly responsible for these two areas, but he will frequently be required to put in the legwork and liaise between the sponsoring company, the club and the Press. This tends to happen because the coach has more time to attend to this role than anybody else, and in the main it is of particular concern to him that the teams are run both efficiently and viably.

It is never easy to define just where the role of the coach finishes and that of the club manager begins. The coach is normally entrusted with all aspects of the playing side and that often includes organisation. While the coach may willingly adopt the organisation of the teams, he may often be required to handle the club's internal leagues and competitions as well, so it is quite helpful if he has the backing of the manager. The manager's added experience of raising commercial interest should help in the task of paying for these events, but it is undisputed that the club coach should also be involved. In this area of collaboration with the manager, the coach should see himself as an agent for selling squash to the membership. He should, furthermore, intensify the interest already evident when he is preaching to the converted. This regard for the public relations aspect of the coach's job tends to separate the good coaches from the ordinary ones. And a coach who is highly respected in this area is likely to be in demand from a number of clubs.

The coach can have a decided influence on the amount of members in a club by virtue of his ability in the public relations field and, in co-operation with the manager, he can plan events that will further attract members and even non-members to the club. In this category, for example, is the exhibition match or the prize presentation dinner, the squash club tour or coaching courses for visitors. The scope is endless to the coach with a bit of imagination. The public relations aspect of the job can be further extended if the coach is sufficiently respected to be offered a column in the local newspaper or perhaps a regular spot on the local radio station. At no stage should the coach fight shy of such opportunities.

The club membership will often turn to their coach for advice on their equipment as well as on the playing aspects, and thus the coach may have the chance to look after the club shop. This tends to depend upon the coach's aptitude for shopkeeping and it does not suit the taste of every individual; but it is undoubtedly an opportunity for him to offer an added facility to the club, bearing in mind that he will have more expertise than most in selecting rackets and other equipment. It is foolish for the coach to refuse to take full advantage of this facility without due consideration – after all, whether the coach runs the shop or not, he will still be expected to give advice to members on the choice of equipment.

The club will form the main area of work for the coach, but in recent times the S.R.A. has developed further schemes to offer the ambitious player at whatever level the chance to link with players of the same ilk at national and regional levels. This forms an incentive to an elitist scheme from which national teams can be selected, and at the last count the S.R.A. were running squads from national under-10 to under-19 levels inclusive, which also encompass the age groups at under-12, under-14 and under-16. Further on there is a series of events for players at under-23 level and ultimately the older players can play age-group events at over-35, over-45 (veterans) and over-55 (vintage). These age-group categories frequently meet for squad training and coaching sessions and some of them run full national teams at the respective levels. Naturally there is an increasing need for coaches to work in this framework, so the role for coaches is developing on a freelance basis – although in some of these areas the requirement is more for quality players to provide opposition and give advice rather than specific coaching.

One exceedingly visionary scheme of coaching has been developed. It is called the North-Eastern Centre of Excellence and provides specific assistance as the name indicates, while at the same time being at pains to cater across the age span, predominantly at junior level – under-19 – and incorporating girls as well as boys. The concept has two key aspects. One is the particular efficiency with which the organisation runs, and credit in this respect is due both to the ruling squash body in the

Hiddy Jahan, a player of vast experience, encouraging a younger team member in the Ardleigh Hall match against Dunnings Mill of East Grinstead in the American Express National League. Ardleigh Hall in their first season in the National League, used their blend of youth and experience to great effect

area and also to Malcolm Willstrop and his resident team of coaches, who set the schedules for the scheme. The other enlightened aspect in that players who have passed through the scheme are encouraged to return to put back what they have taken out and to add a lively presence to a good squash environment. This all helps to improve standards. It would be an optimistic sign to see more schemes of its kind in operation, but for the coach there are always targets at which to aim his more successful players and it is his responsibility to do so.

The coach is essential to the sport. He is its life's blood and represents its future by fostering the interest of both young and new players. It is to this area that the sport must turn for its future well-being.

9. Match preparation and psychology

Now that we have reviewed all the elements that combine to make up the physical side of squash, it is time to take a look at the way in which these are bonded together for success by the player's own psychological make-up. It is virtually impossible to produce the correct mental attitudes by coaching alone, although that is not to say that the player cannot be influenced towards them. In the long run, however, it is the player's own problem, for he enters the court alone and stands or falls according to his ability, both physical and – particularly – mental. It is the expression of the player's own personality, exuberant or reserved, that will determine the end-product seen by onlookers. Put another way, all the strokes which the player demonstrates tactically will fundamentally require a strong basic will to win. It is the quality of this will to win that becomes obvious, and it is often shown by the player's determination, resilience, resourcefulness and reluctance to part with points.

Motivation

Perhaps it is stating the obvious, but there are few players who relish the prospect of losing a match, and this is the strongest motivating factor of all. All players have matches which are of special importance to them. Just as everybody can dream of lifting the trophy at the final of the British Open, so can players of all the different playing standards regard certain matches. As soon as a player consciously decides which particular event is to be viewed as his ultimate aim, he will reserve his most important motivation of the season for his efforts to attain this goal. It may be the club tournament, in the local leagues as part of a team, the handicap tournament, the county championship, or the ultimate of the World Open; but it is the fear of losing in this special event which has particular meaning for the individual and can produce either a positive or negative effect on him.

The most evident effect brought about by this fear is that the player works harder to try to achieve a positive improvement in his performance. This is the best possible effect and is usually the outward indication of the good match player with a reliable temperament. On the other hand there is the player who will become nervous and anxious and therefore unable to give of his best. He has a habit of leaving his best form behind on the practice court. In the first instance the player will naturally find himself facing fewer problems, but in the latter case the player will cause his coach considerable distress as he tries to discover the best means of making the player do himself justice. This brief comparison provides an insight into the problems of the psychology of a squash player.

Pre-match routines

There are few players who have not experienced some difficulties in trying to achieve the right attitude with which to enter the court. The solution can never be straightforward and is also never definitive, but there are ways and means of trying to improve the psychological preparation for match play. There is no doubt that the player can help himself by analysing his situation carefully and creating good habits and a routine to which he can adhere before, during and after every match. These habits will be studied as the chapter unfolds, but at the

Andrew Foley and Andrew Danzey of the Nottingham club spin the racket for the right to serve at the start of their match

moment it is sufficient to say that the establishment of a routine helps the player to feel confidence in his own ability to perform well and to achieve the result he desires.

The way in which a player builds up to a match plays an integral role in putting him into the right psychological frame of mind when he steps into the court. In this chapter we are going to examine the preparations for a match and investigate the habits which will hopefully become an intrinsic part of the routine for playing the match. It should be assumed that the player is about to play a match which is of great significance to his season, so he will quite naturally have prepared himself by the use of the practice sessions which have already been discussed, and may indeed have spent the previous week concentrating on something similar to the schedule outlined in the working model suggested in Chapter 6.

The great importance of practising in this way is that it develops a form of discipline in the player which becomes his incentive for always trying to improve himself and his skills. The object in this instance is for the player to derive from the practice a high degree of confidence with which to enter the court for his big match. This confidence should stem from the fact that the strokes which may be required to ensure a win will have been rehearsed time and time again and, hopefully, perfected. This should mean that when the opportunity arises to play the strokes during the match, such confidence will have become so innate that it allows the player to seize that chance. It is far easier said than done. Nevertheless, the lesson is especially worthwhile. Happy then will be the player who makes his errors on the practice court and gets them out of his system so that he can grasp his chance to play the strokes correctly in the context of a match. The player who fails miserably in the match, but excels himself on the practice court, will be less contented. The need for confidence is essential to both these players and the habit of thorough and regular practice is of paramount importance to their match preparations.

Each individual will approach his practice and his match play in his own way, but there are still areas of common ground, in which all players' overall attitude must reflect similar traits. These characteristics are particularly notable in the work that precedes a match. It will be assumed that the player will have assiduously applied himself to a schedule or a working model in the physical build-up to the match, and it is hoped that this will leave him feeling confident about his stroke play and his physical condition as he prepares himself for the final build-up. It is further assumed that the player will have taken on board the relevant fuel to feed the engine of his squash performance, by following a well-balanced diet. As the player continues his physical preparations, it is important in the time just before his match that he reduces his workload and makes a positive attempt to seek sufficient rest for the exertions ahead.

Psychologically the rest should heighten the player's appetite for the match in prospect by depriving him of his regular workload. This period of time is frequently referred to as 'tapering' and is important because it allows the player to arrive for the match hungry, rested and in a relaxed frame of mind, so avoiding any unnecessary nervous tensions. Quite often the player who has another career will try to take time off work to make sure that these final preparations of rest and relaxation are well met. To the player with an active mind, it may be a tough proposition to spend the last twenty-four hours before a match involved in the so-called winding-down before the final build-up; nevertheless it is important that the time is well spent relaxing rather than nervously awaiting the match and anxiously increasing mental unrest and pressures. This period can be extremely difficult to organise and some players counter the problem by going to the cinema, watching the television, reading a book, listening to music or even playing cards. All these activities keep the player occupied. They represent a complete break from his practice routine and are not especially tiring physically. It is imperative that each individual player should find his own preferred activities which will put him into the right frame of mind.

The day of the match

It is clearly beneficial if a player can manage a good night's sleep before the big day, but, all things being equal, this may not be as easy as it sounds. When players do take too early a night on the eve of a match, they may toss and turn and sleep only fitfully. It is far better for the player to wait until he feels tired before going to bed and trying to sleep right through, and much more likely to ensure a relaxed frame of mind.

After a light breakfast on the day of the match, the player will be advised to take a gentle practice session, designed merely to loosen himself up and to prepare for the events to come. It is again sensible not to overdo such practice. The main objective is for him to 'feel' the ball on the racket, build up a nice rhythm in the stroke, run out any stiffness that there may be in the muscles and do some light movement that will inspire confidence rather than produce a state of fatigue.

When this has been achieved, the player can take some light lunch, resting assured that he knows the time of his match and that he has his equipment clean and ready. The player's attitude towards the simple chores, such as clean kit and punctuality in arriving for his match, speak volumes about his overall approach and his desire to win. Quite often this attitude is the mark of the potential of the player. This is because the best player will quite simply leave nothing to chance in preparing himself thoroughly and absolutely to perform at his best and achieve the right result.

After the pre-match lunch the player will again have a chance to relax and calm himself, probably passing his time in his chosen recreational activities, before going to the court in the evening. All his activities on the day of the match should be geared towards keeping himself as free from harassment and tension as possible, bearing in mind that the game itself may well be full of this kind of aggravation in a squash context. The aim is for the player to start the match feeling fresh and calm and therefore able to cope with his situation from the outset. He may even be prepared to hazard a guess at what examinations may lie in store on court. Pre-match practice on the court which has been scheduled for the match itself should give the player the feel of the impending atmosphere as well as an opportunity to become accustomed to the bounce of the ball and the colour of the lights, floor and walls, especially if the match should be taking place on a glass or perspex transparent court. It will be useful for the player to take such data into the match itself, and it should be stored as experience rather than regarded as a distraction when the prime requirement will be to play well.

It will be noted that so far a general routine of match preparation has emerged without making anything too specific. This routine will be further shaped by each individual, who will bring his own personality to bear, and follow his own personal idiosyncracies, all of which will be no less valid or out of place. A coach can merely advise and create guidelines in these areas, for in the end the player is the one who needs to be happy with his preparations. The coach, therefore, will encourage the player to analyse his own motives and personality, and hope to originate and encourage the right preparations in the pre-match build-up.

The player must take care to time his arrival at the club so that he has enough scope to continue his preparations once he has arrived, and finally complete them so that he is happy to take the court at the appointed start. This may well entail taking into account any possible traffic problems en route. At this point the player should be as in control of his pre-match destiny as is attainable. If that is not the case, then he must reappraise his habits and not be afraid to seek advice from players who are vastly experienced in such situations and may have something constructive in terms of help to offer. This may well be the time for the player to take good ideas from those who are willing to share them, and to adapt them to suit himself.

The next step, however, is the beginning of the moment of truth and it is now solely in the player's hands as to whether he passes or fails the test. There can be no harsher an assessor than the game of squash for in the final analysis the player is in isolation. Those walls may now appear to be part of those original prison cells that are said to have given birth to the concept of squash! Again the coach can merely offer advice and try to encourage his charge to think constantly about how best to deploy his forces to exploit any weaknesses in the enemy's armoury.

Frequently the battle commences in the changing room; some players are noted for their gift of the gab and will chat in a way calculated to dismantle the confidence that their opponents may have built up. Alternatively players may try to lull their opponents into a false sense of security with talk about their own poor form and bad results. The player may have to contend with all of this kind of chicanery. There is nothing simpler as an attempt to influence the build-up to the match than an opponent who looks smart, carries a bundle of rackets or sports a healthy sun-tan to give the impression of immense physical strength. In no circumstances should the player allow himself to be taken in by such ploys. He should quite simply be aware of the possibilities and perhaps, where appropriate and quite legitimate, seek to make the most of such opportunities himself. The match itself will be as much, if not more, a battle of personalities and willpower as a test of stroke-making and physical conditioning.

The knock-up is the first chance for the player to assess his opponent, unless he has seen him in action on other occasions. Even if he has, it is useful to appraise the opponent again because the mood of the moment and his current form, as with the player himself, will make him a different proposition on each occasion that they meet. Such basic aspects as a player's left-handedness, his favourite strokes and his glaring weaknesses, should be sought for storage in the memory bank.

When the match begins, the player must have a clear idea of what he is setting out to achieve, taking full advantage of any useful information that he has discerned about his opponent so that he can be more alert. Of primary importance to the player is the reaffirmation of his will to win and the method or match plan, taking into account the relevant factors and observations by which he is attempting to gain victory. It does no harm to appraise the opponent and try to work out the strategy that he will adopt. Then comes the contest as to whose strategy is the better founded and ultimately the more successful. It is absolutely essential that the player should concentrate totally on his squash and be willing to switch tactics and think constantly about varying his attack. An alert mind and competent strokes, allied to physical conditioning, are the means to good squash. The player must try to settle into a rhythm of tactics and strokemaking to challenge the best reserves of his opponent. Once this rhythm is struck, the player should find that he will accumulate points and games as long as his concentration is maintained. The old axiom 'Never change a winning game' must be uppermost in his mind.

If, on the other hand, the player should find himself on the wrong end of the match, then he should seek by any legitimate means to disrupt the rhythm that his opponent has established. In simple terms, if the opponent is winning points by severe low and hard hitting, then it is inappropriate for the player to continue playing as he has been doing. Rather the answer may lie in the change of pace to the slow ball lobbed high. The opponent will then find himself with more time to make his plays and think about what he is doing rather than playing instinctively, which has been the key to his success. This slowing down of an opponent will force him to generate the pace of the ball by his efforts alone and this may just do enough to disturb his accuracy.

Match techniques and psychology

At the start of the match the player should go about his task solidly rather than spectacularly, except on a day when his confidence and self-belief are running extremely high, but in normal circumstances it is quite important to lay down to an opponent the terms on which the match is to be played. Unforced errors are not desirable because they will culminate in an opponent running up too great a lead at the outset so that it becomes a monumental task for the player to haul himself back into a strong position. When the player starts solidly, he will put his opponent to the task at once and there is every chance that the opponent will then get off to a bad start.

Ideally, the player should initially be able to stay in the middle of the court as a result of his good play to the back-court areas. He should then await the loose return to finish in the front-court area. This will cause the opponent considerable problems in retrieving the strokes. Wherever possible it should give the opponent the feeling of perpetual motion with no opportunity to play his best strokes, so that he will begin to believe that it is only a matter of time before he runs out of energy. The player should have a strong desire to dominate his opponent and, in situations in which his ball control is good enough, to send him chasing the ball as if it were being dangled on the end of a piece of string. Incorporated in this wish to dominate, the player will also have a masochistic desire to endure the same type of domination from his opponent, but always at heart preferring the former to the latter. The margin of difference betwen the two may on occasions be tangible in the match result of ten-nine in the fifth and deciding game.

A severe example of mental domination may be examined by reference to the match between Geoff Hunt and Jonah Barrington in the British Open final of 1972. After losing the first game love-nine, Barrington attacked a weakness of Hunt – or rather an area of less strength – by continually striking the ball high to Hunt's backhand side. it was the only part of the court in which Hunt was not to able to create enormous pressure on Barrington. Although this tactic was not successful at once, it had the effect of lengthening the rallies and taking the sting out of what had been a venomous attack on Barrington up to that point in the match. In the end it was enough to tip the balance of the match to a long and hard-fought win by a very narrow margin for Barrington. What had looked to be a potentially comfortable win for Hunt was wrested from him by Barrington's complete control of his mental discipline – a key aspect of a player's game. Barrington has long been noted as a player with outstanding mastery of his own squash abilities, and it was this unyielding strength that was communicated to Hunt on this occasion.

The true psychological qualities of a player are more likely to be revealed on the occasions on which he finds himself two games to love in arrears. Every player will find himself in this situation at one time or another, but, far from being despondent,

Jonah Barrington had some 'brutal battles' with Geoff Hunt to determine the World Championship and the limits of human endurance, skill and determination were reached in the pursuit of this ultimate honour

he should take heart from the fact that many games have been won from two games to love down and, what is more, frequently from match ball down as well. The overriding lesson to be learnt is that no match is over until the final point has been won or lost. Even that may sometimes be disputed on a let call, so the player must maintain his concentration until the bitter end. There was even one occasion when one of the players in a match had reached the changing room, believing that he had won, and was then recalled to the court by the referee to play a let ball. Needless to say this had such a disruptive effect on the player's concentration that he was then unable to complete the match in his favour. The fact that matches can be won in such circumstances should prove to be a great source of encouragement to the player to work harder and to fight back whenever he is confronted by a deficit. It is never ideal to have to face such situations, but there are times when the good form of an opponent or the poor form of the player himself require the mental capacity to stage such recoveries.

The player should be aware that the personal steel of his ambition makes it possible for him to play badly – not deliberately, of course – but still be capable of winning. In fact, it will be

Gawain Briars, a British National Champion and World ranked, has sometimes failed to deliver his best form in the most prestigious events such as the British Open. Some pundits would argue that it is a deficiency in his temperament

becoming more and more clear that the squash player faces his most severe mental examination when he has to cope with the hardships of adversity on the occasions when all the pre-match planning goes awry.

The nature of the sport is such that even the laws state that play must be continuous and, with the speed of the ball and the reactions to deal with it, there are ample opportunities for errors to be made because any player is not entirely in control of what is happening to him. It is this which builds resilience in a player and produces the attitude that 'Every rally is a new rally and needs to be played on its own merits, not on the basis of what has gone before.' It is also useful to take this attitude a stage further and apply the same concept to every stroke, because it has the effect of causing the player to consider all his options. Hopefully, such reflections will reinforce the best frame of mind in the player and maintain the right level of concentration.

At some stage of his career the player will face the further test of losing his form – the ability to play well naturally – and this can be a particularly trying time. The best advice is for even more critical, but constructive, self-analysis in all areas of the game. It is significant that the player may well be able to trace the problems in his game to corresponding difficulties in his personal or working life. As such they are especially distracting and the severity of the match pressure which the player has to endure leaves no scope for any diversions, otherwise the ultimate result will be a disaster.

Nevertheless, there are two ways in which a player can cope with a loss of form. The first is to take a complete break or a holiday, or even concentrate purely and simply on tackling the source of the problem as it is known. The second way is to redouble practice and training efforts to restore good habits and try to accumulate an increasing amount of confidence. Constant examination of all the player's methods should lead to an improvement, certainly of preparation and hopefully of performance. Inevitably the player will not be at the peak of his performance continuously, and he must adopt a philosophical attitude to cope with the ups and downs of any sporting career. The sooner he develops such an approach, the sooner the trauma of setbacks will be overcome. Needless to say, it is no use crying over spilt milk; a defeat should be constructively and practically analysed, and a learning process should follow from this analysis so that the player can look forward more optimistically to the next match as soon as possible.

Gawain Briars discussing the referee's interpretation of the rules. Gawain's technique is such that he is rarely in his opponent's way and thus the let count against him is normally low. There are other world ranked players who are more obstructive

Dean Williams is a colourful Australian player who has the ability to make a referee's life difficult with his instant wit and repartee and clever exploitation of circumstances to his own advantage

Just as a loss of form is a source of difficulty for the player, so can be the victory, since it is very easy for him to become complacent by basking in the afterglow of a good performance. There is no place for complacency. The best players seek consistency in their performances as well as the ability to reach a peak for the major events, so it is calmness and control of a player's emotions which are his biggest asset.

This should be particularly borne in mind in terms of refereeing decisions. Refereeing, as in all sports, is an extremely difficult job and, as a result, any bad refereeing decisions against the player should be accepted impassively as often as possible. On the occasions when a player allows bad decisions to distract him, the consequences are likely to be calamitous. When Peter Chalk was the manager of the British team, he was so concerned about such possibilities that he insisted that referees should deliberately give bad decisions against members of the team in practice. The idea was to give them the opportunity to learn how to cope with such situations and that, chastened by this experience, the players should be thoroughly prepared for any eventuality and would respond in the right manner.

The art of gamesmanship is another examination of the player's temperament and it is again his responsibility to learn how to cope with the situations which occasionally transgress the bounds of legality. There are, of course, some shrewd exponents of gamesmanship, who do not actually break the laws of the game, but cause sufficient disruptions to present the player with a problem, and often this is a situation with which referees are unable to contend. The player will again overcome this problem thanks to high levels of concentration, adhering singlemindedly to his main purpose and avoiding the temptation to become involved in any way. It benefits the opponent greatly if the player joins in the chit-chat, thereby allowing himself to be distracted. It must be emphasised that it is not the policy of this book to advocate gamesmanship other than by ruses that are entirely within the framework of the laws of the game. It is as well for the player to be aware that disrupting his opponent's rhythm of play is desirable, especially if it is successful, but this should be achieved only by cunning tactical play and not by backchat.

The player's performance is a direct function of the control that he exerts over his stroke play by his mental application. This, like every other human characteristic, has frailties and

Dean Williams of Australia inspects the wood on Qamar Zaman's racket after the latter had hit a lucky shot. Such a situation may have been designed to gain the tiring Australian a breather and distract his opponent, as well as entertain the crowd

these are often influenced by moods of one sort or another. It is far from easy to perform consistently to a high degree of quality, but it is important that this is the goal which is continually sought. Much of the player's performance will be further influenced by his personality type in terms of the kind of game that suits him best and which he opts to play. Obviously the attritional and defensive player will not be as inconsistent as a more adventurous strokemaker, though the rewards for the strokemaker may be potentially greater.

It is a mark of Qamar Zaman's ability that he managed to combine a high degree of innovatory stroke play with a large amount of consistency, always giving the impression of supreme confidence. This is especially awe-inspiring and presents a difficult psychological obstacle for the opponent to overcome. More recently Jahangir Khan, the world champion, has inspired tremendous respect and overawed his nearest rivals by the seeming ease with which he varies his tactics and is still invincible on a background of exceptional physical conditioning. Psychologically the rivals feel his invincibility to such an extent that they are hard-pressed to discern any weaknesses that he may or may not have. Jahangir's domination may continue indefinitely until a player who has not come under his exceptional psychological stranglehold will appear. He will then set about tackling the more immediate problems of trying to find Jahangir's weaknesses and so plot his downfall. It is quite possible that this player is not even on the world tour at this stage.

Jahangir's domination leads on to the concept of a player playing against an opponent, not his reputation. If a player can so dominate his opponent, then in the end the aura may well be enough to cause a player to beat himself. Such self-doubt in a player is primary suicide and is totally at variance with the positive aspects involved in preparing him for his matches. It is vital that the player estimates the proposition of playing squash against his opponent, and not against the previous achievements of that opponent. It is essential for a player to believe that he is only as good as his last match and this must be a source of encouragement in every respect.

Many players will suffer the greatest problems with their stroke play as a result of the psychological factor, and it is through the release of psychological inhibition that the player is able to get the best out of his strokes and tackle the problem of winning his match with conviction. It has often been said that squash attempts to create a state of controlled violence and that this is some modern-day re-creation of primeval animal instincts. This perhaps underlines the complexity of the processes which are taking place in the mind of a player during his match. It is the total disciplining of the player's mind that *per se* will control the course of the match, and it will not be until the very last point of the match has been won – perhaps two hours or more – that the final release will be obtained. The player can then ease off and set about unwinding so that he can relax once again, having released all his tensions and frustrations, and hopefully savour the sweet taste of success.

10. A summary and a look to the future

John Le Lievre of Guernsey after winning a close-fought match with Peter Hill of Singapore. This match seems to have given both these talented players some satisfaction!

In the same way as the players, whether victor or vanquished, make their way to the changing room at the end of a match to wash away the sweat of their toils and clean up to face their normal every-day lives again, so we can do the same here. The final objective in the afterglow of the match is for the player to benefit from the experience and learn the main lessons. The book has

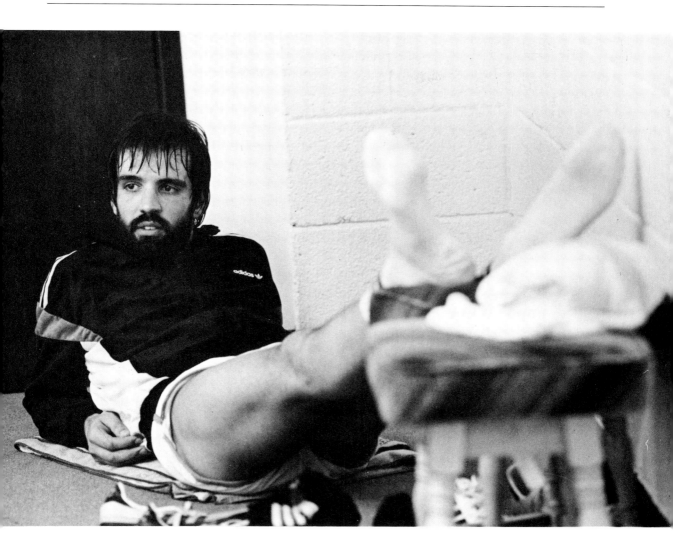

John Le Lievre relaxes in the changing room after his match with Peter Hill. Perhaps fatigue has set in and the realisation has dawned that there is another match to play in the tournament

been moulded into the shape of a match by considering the preparations and background, and now the conclusions must be drawn.

The game of squash can be loosely divided into two areas of learning – its basic foundations, and the opportunity for the individual to show some self-expression within it. The game is all-embracing in terms of stroke play, physical conditioning and mental approach. In considering its overall potential, the accents have been placed in specific areas that may or may not be recognisable to players in the game; but roughly speaking it represents an approach that provides many alternatives and encourages the player to solve many of the game's problems for himself. Equally it is hoped that the basics have been covered in such a way that they both contain a common denominator and offer a good launching-pad for the individual to choose his own style and methods. The basic ideal is that the game can be all things to all people, and this approach is to be encouraged. It has been to squash's detriment that many club players have felt that the game would not necessarily offer them a great deal of success without total commitment and dedication. Suffice it to say that squash has a well-defined role to play for those who merely want to enjoy it, but in seeking that enjoyment it is no less important for the player to be concerned with learning more about the game and trying to raise standards. There is no doubt that by learning about the game a player will increase his enjoyment factor, and to do this it is necessary for him to commit himself to strict and obsessive regimes of practice and training.

It is hoped that in the preceding chapters the emphasis has been placed firmly on educating for enjoyment and improvement, and that it has been left to the individual to decide upon the degree of commitment that he has to the game. At the two different ends of the scale are the people who will organise their working lives to fit in with their squash requirements and those who plan their social lives – and playing – around squash club activities. The object has been to lay the same basic framework and learning programme for all participants, in the same way that a golfer would not merely be given a putter with which to play a round of golf.

Among the vast number of players there will be many who have had little or no coaching and who will, therefore, have worked out much of the game by commonsense and more general sporting instincts. It is on these players, who are often quite competent, that there has been a reflection concerning the very basic technical requirements. This is because the advancement of skills can be handicapped by the poor foundations on which the player has had to build. In simple terms, it is easy for the player to arrive at the ball with only one option. Much more difficult, but far more productive, is the ability to arrive at the ball with several options and then select the right one for the purposes of winning the rally. This may be old hat to many, but it is the term of reference which is especially important when a player is trying to develop a greater capacity for strokemaking and, therefore, the expansion of tactical options. The game becomes decidedly more interesting with this extra facility, but it is dependent purely and simply on having the right grounding. Here it has not been the intention to dwell in detail upon aspects of technique that may be long-winded and complicated, but particularly to emphasise the starting-point and its relevance to progress.

The player should now seek to enjoy the increased arsenal of strokes at his disposal; the great fascination of the game is the tactical employment of them against a variety of different opponents. This is the time when the sport becomes all-embracing as it includes the aspects of both mental and physical agility.

There is not much fun in slogging the ball relentlessly around the court with no real accuracy except the realisation that the player packs the determination to seek a high level of fatigue and release of tension and pent-up emotions. It is amazing how often players of this ilk are to be seen in squash clubs testing the success of brute force and ignorance. Furthermore, it is significant that many of these players are merely waiting for the right advice so that they can develop the skills which elude them purely because they have been self-taught. It is remarkable how far a player can develop on his own, especially if he selects a wide and varied range of opponent. It is also intrinsic to the sport that players learn from playing each other, but in the final analysis the player will fall short when confronted by a more educated opponent unless he is particularly perceptive at working things out for himself.

In the tactical context the emphasis lies most desirably in setting no limits on different combinations of strokes which provide the means of winning rallies. Much responsibility in this area lies in the ingenuity of the player and also in his greater willingness to search for the original and most effective ways of accumulating points. The scope in this context can be infinite to a player of some imagination, but it cannot be denied that there will be players who prefer to restrict their strokemaking capacity and to play to an efficient and disciplined tactical plan. This is no less valid, but it is for the player to decide which methods are best suited to his personal requirements. The objective is to place all options at the player's disposal and then provide him with the ability to be discerning, play to his strengths and harness them in such a way as to gain success. The player must decide where his interests lie and then he must work hard to ensure that the methods function. No matter what the player's decision, there is one factor which unites all the participants and that is the need for them to practise hard to make sure that they are capable of playing in the manner which they have chosen. This is the most obvious difference between success and failure.

The more diverse and expansive the player decides to be, the more he will need to perfect his ball control and his concentration to encompass the higher degree of risks he may take. On the other hand, the player who opts to operate on a restricted plan will gain his success as a result of the virtues of patience and attrition. Plainly the players who fall between these two categories will need to blend such qualities.

It is noteworthy that the chosen examples tend to polarise these qualities, but this is misleading and should be regarded as some sort of licence for the purposes of example. After all, it is important to be aware that all the qualities mentioned are required in a player's make-up, but that they are more evident in one type than in another. The message is loud and clear: practice and hard work are the sole means to success; and that success can be quantified in terms of what the player puts in, the player gets out. This view is not intended to be off-putting for the social player, but merely to express a fundamental learning requirement.

At the beginner stage the players are only too happy to work hard in order to get to grips with their game. This never diminishes. There can be an element of tedium inherent in practice exercises and training methods, but again in keeping with the overall aim of this book, it is intended that the player should bring an inquisitive and imaginative attitude to learning the game and seek as many varied ways as possible of practising skills that are repetitive by their very nature. This can be only a source of inspiration to a player who maintains a high level of practice in the game.

There have already been suggestions for a comprehensive selection of practice exercises and routines, and an actual schedule, with the aim of preparing a player for his matches. In keeping with the spirit of these, it is always a good idea to assess the variety and seek to adapt the routines for the benefit of the player's greater interest, but not at the expense of restricting himself to practising merely 'the favourite things' which are usually his strengths. The programme should balance between these strengths and solid endeavour to improve weaknesses. Often in the early stages players will seek to avoid the backhand side of the court, but such action will lead only to taking them down a cul-de-sac, because the player will eventually have that weakness ruthlessly exploited. This can be demoralising and lead to stagnancy as the player comes to terms with the fact that he must try to erase that weakness.

It is the player's capacity for self-analysis and honest appraisal that will provide him with the opportunity to practise diligently to improve his game. In this regard, the player will be well advised to seek guidance, experience, motivation and encouragement from a coach at various intervals, if not more regular assistance. If this facility is not available, then the same function can often be performed by the club champion or fellow team members who might sometimes be willing to help – though it must be stressed that the discerning player will be aware of the fact that on occasion the more ambitious types may well offer misinformation with a view to his demise!

This book is intended to prepare the player and make him sufficiently inquisitive to be able to decipher the information available to him. The role of a coach, especially a good one, is never to be underestimated since it is true that in specific terms the game still provides plenty to learn. In a wider sense, the pattern of matches played and their tactical shapes are changing and are most likely to be taken into new dimensions at the highest levels. It is especially relevant to remember that the game is still relatively new and unexplored in this sense.

There are no frontiers for the player in getting to know himself though the medium of the game of squash rackets. The all-embracing challenges insist that as the player achieves a higher degree of competence, so will he acquire a greater knowledge of his own personality traits and be able to recognise how he copes with pressure in the broadest sense of the word. The essence of the game is the thirst for increased self-knowledge, and because of squash's comparative newness the context of this self-discovery is not so clearly defined as in the more established sports. Squash is a new opportunity and thus has a particular place in the modern life-style. The sport is developing at a significant rate and it is to the future that we must now turn.

It has, after all, taken squash just those few years since 1969 for the court to develop from a box of four white-plastered walls to the current portable 'goldfish bowl' which is the requirement for top international events. Seating capacity has escalated from twenty or thirty people leaning over a balcony to three thousand in a proper auditorium. But as yet the television companies have neglected to do anything but scratch the surface of covering the sport. It is significant that it took a similar period of time for the coverage of snooker in 'Pot Black' to transform the sport from the occasional half-an-hour's coverage on a black and white programme to the point of extensive – and arguably saturation – coverage which is now the norm. The solution to snooker's difficulties was naturally the development of colour television. It is possible that the problems of squash coverage are of a similar kind and that they require a similar period of coming to terms with the difficulties, but at the same time there is no doubt that sooner or later squash will appear regularly on the TV screen.

In the eyes of the television companies the sport poses problems in conveying the real action and drama of events. The world's top squash players make the game seem deceptively easy. As would be expected, they are extremely well-tuned athletes and so it is not easy to discern the physical problems that a club player experiences. The speed of the ball means that it is difficult to see (although the new dimpled ball will undoubtedly improve this situation). There is also the fact that the ball is not struck to an easily defined goal. In comparison with ice hockey, for example, in which the puck travels at similar speeds to the squash ball, it does, however, have a particular target, in other words, the back of the net. The equivalent target in squash would probably be the nick, but this is not nearly as easily identifiable. Furthermore, to the mass audience and the less educated viewer, the sport will eventually seem to revolve round the players making errors and the one who makes the fewer errors will win. This is far from healthy for the presentation of the sport because it is a great deal more exciting to view the positive conclusion of a rally.

This situation can be overcome by good presentation and lucid commentary work so that the uninitiated are able to learn more about the tactics and methods of the game taking place before their very eyes. Accordingly, they will learn to appreciate that the rally is won more often by a player outmanoeuvring his opponent and perceive how pressure has been built up to a point where, although the opponent may get his racket to the ball, he is not capable of actually returning it.

It is this insight into the sport that produces the fascination, but, as in all sports, such understanding comes only as the onlookers learn the finer points. Essentially no sport is good entertainment if the spectators do not understand what is going on. But squash can most certainly be considered as good spectator entertainment, if only because an audience of about three thousand viewed the final of the 1985 British Open, even though

The 'televisible' ball is similar in appearance to a golf ball. Reflective material is set in the dimples to reflect bright light, thus its appearance on television is similar to that of the blimp on a space invader machine. This is one of the technological advances which will help to enhance the mass appeal of the sport

it was relatively one-sided, as is often the case in major championships.

Perhaps the final area of improvement in which squash can prepare itself for television coverage might come from within the confines of the sport itself, with particular reference to the court. It has seen considerable development so far, but there are perhaps more advances still that would make it more presentable to the television cameras. There are inherent problems attached to a glass or perspex wall built in a free-standing manner. It needs support because of its considerable weight, so the various fins that support the 'goldfish bowl' have tended to make the court seem a little bit like a Meccano set. Most recently the squash powers-that-be have enhanced the court's aesthetic appearance by colouring the floor dark blue, making the lines yellow and playing with a white-coloured ball. This is all quite feasible against the milky grey colour of the transparent walls and such colouring has enlivened the court's appearance on the screen by avoiding the singularly boring contast of a black ball on white walls. This aspect is predominantly cosmetic and there is no doubt that as the powers-that-be wrestle further with presenting the sport for television coverage, such changes will continue to find the most aesthetic blend of presentation.

There have also been attempts to look at the scoring systems utilised for televised matches. The current situation involving hand-in and hand-out is largely incomprehensible at times to the mass audience, so the American system has been adopted in which play is determined by a point at the end of every rally. There has also been some speculation about the number of points that may comprise a game, such options being nine, eleven, thirteen or fifteen. But there has been no conclusive proof at this stage that it has led to any major improvement in the game for mass audiences, so the original structure has been maintained for the time being.

Squash has developed considerably in its short history and, more importantly, will progress further in the future. It is easy to overlook its background historically and expect it to stand alongside older and more established sports as accepted television viewing. But the myth that squash is not a spectator sport has already been laid to rest in terms of live action at major events and it is only a matter of time before this is translated to television coverage as well.

The other significant development of squash has been the increase in its appeal worldwide. It is no longer simply the domain of a handful of founder members of the International Squash Rackets' Federation, for at the last count it had spread to almost fifty countries in total. The original expansion of squash from England was largely achieved by the expatriate community. But although this may have set the pattern in the early days, the enlargement of the squash community as a whole has stemmed from the fact that the sport is a very convenient one and is widely available to the traveller; and it is such travellers who have fostered an enthusiasm for squash on their expanding routes around the world. Accordingly, as world travel increases, so do the interests of the sport.

There is one slight contradiction to this, which exists in America and, to a lesser extent, in Canada. In these countries there is a game of the same name, but which has some different equipment. The court is narrower and has different line markings, while the ball, which is called the seventy-plus, is harder. Essentially there is a difference in the method of scoring, which is known as the American system, but it is not completely alien to worldwide squash enthusiasts because it is used in the doubles game. The American game puts a premium on fast reactions and hard hitting with the ball travelling quicker because it is harder.

At one time there was little transfer of players from the softball game to the American hard-ball counterpart, but, in keeping with the development of squash as a whole, Jahangir Khan is currently the world champion at both types. As might be expected with a developing sport, the two games are coming closer, and rightly so because in the final analysis it seems that squash players may well play regularly at both and merely view the problem in the same way as tennis players do when they change back and forth from the different surfaces of their courts.

There is no doubt that the policies of squash development as a whole will benefit from both games working together. There is a consideration that the American game is less physically demanding and this theory is probably substantiated by the fact that the legendary Hashim Khan has played this to a ripe old age. He still plays occasionally, but he may have found that the rigours of the soft-ball game were a little too much for him. But inevitably at the highest levels the physical demands of both codes will be considerable and should not be underestimated. Canada is a most interesting country to study in terms of such squash development because it was originally a stronghold of

Jan Ulf Soderberg, the Swedish Number 1

There have been many notable
Egyptian players. Here is Ali Aziz,
who changed his nationality to
Swedish to maintain his top 20 ranking
in the world

Ross Norman, New Zealand Number 1
and World Number 2, recovered from a
horrific parachuting accident to
continue his top level squash career.
Though he is from New Zealand he is
now based in England, near Heathrow
Airport

Stuart Davenport, another New
Zealand player who emerged rapidly
onto the world scene and now ranks
amongst the top 10

the hard-ball game with little, if any, of the soft-ball variety being
played. But it has seen the development of the soft-ball to such
an extent that there is now almost an equal measure of both and
the two games seem to lie quite happily side by side.

There have been some notable developments of squash overall
in countries in which the sport was hitherto relatively unknown
and the astounding feature has been the short period of time involved. One obvious example is Sweden, where it has taken
barely a decade for them to create a playing standard that has
made them one of the top two countries in Europe and has

The Guernsey girls: perhaps inspired by John Le Lievre's pioneering squash career, Martine Le Moignan and Lisa Opie reached the highest standards, both just failing to win the British Open at the final hurdle. To produce two ladies who have risen to such heights is an amazing achievement for a tiny island like Guernsey

allowed them to produce at least one player who has been among the top sixteen in the world. Quite clearly there have been other emerging squash nations, but none of them can rival the growth which has taken place in Sweden. At the same time there has been evidence of substantial progress being made most recently in the Far East, which has seen the development of a top world-ranking tournament circuit spanning such places as Singapore, Japan, Hong Kong, Brunei and Malaysia.

There has been considerable interest in Australia as a matter of custom and it is one of the founder playing members of the international federation. More recently New Zealand has been quick to develop the sport. There are also of course the Pakistanis, who obviously form the foremost playing strength of world squash, while the input from Britain must not be forgotten.

Some of the sport's most colourful and skilled performers have hailed from Egypt, where there has been a relatively long history of squash. The local people learnt quite readily from the expatriate beginnings and the sport has since become so popular that the international world championships were held in Egypt in 1985. Other Middle Eastern countries are also beginning to recognise the sport and the early signs indicate that development is imminent.

Europe is already well organised and at the last count almost twenty nations were represented with at least half of them running their own national Open events. Playing visitors from Europe and America are welcome in the Caribbean areas, which should not be overlooked in terms of squash progress. It has been encouraging, especially in view of the climate, to see that the islands have organised several events of international status. Not much further afield in South America there is also evidence of squash activity.

Squash can be considered truly international and, bearing in mind its comparatively brief history, it has developed and spread like the proverbial wild-fire. Assuredly, it has not finished yet. The next phase of the development will inevitably lie in a period of consolidation in the most general sense. More and more people are coming into the sport as raw beginners and it will require a considerable amount of hard work to teach them its many finer points. As a result, the challenge lies firmly in the hands of the coaches, the administrators and the entrepreneurs to improve the standard of play, the leagues, the tournaments and the facilities. Mistakes will have been made from the starting-blocks, especially in the early clubs that were built, but these are bound to be modernised and adapted to suit the changing needs of a better standard of player. Because of the nature of the game it seems that as players develop, they will be more willing to travel to look for different opposition and tournaments in which to test their skills. This does not apply solely at the professional level because there is a great deal of pleasure to be gained from touring at all grades once the player is sufficiently competent. It is, in fact, possible to visualise the day when the framework of squash is as extensive as, if not more so than, the catholic appeal of tennis.

Finally, the sport's great insurance for the future lies in the development of its younger players. Most countries now have well-organised squads for juniors, which start at the under-10 level in England. There will always inevitably be some controversy as to the rights and wrongs of pressing a child into competitive situations at such an early age, but there is nothing wrong with providing an introduction to the sport at such a time and merely setting a course with the rudimentary knowledge. It is wisest then to allow the child's natural enthusiasm to dictate the level of involvement, but at the same time such junior schemes will be a huge source of incentive and pleasure for the child who is highly motivated.

The future of the sport overall would appear to be well founded and it is hoped that there will be a wealth of challenges to the player who determines to undertake them. The accent must always lie on the individual who will get out of the sport only the equivalent of what he puts into it.

The main objective throughout this book has been to raise aspects of the sport for further consideration by the player and to look at existing methods with a fresh approach born out of experience of playing tournament squash at the professional level. Without doubt there will be players and coaches who will differ about the ways in which some of the ideas have been dealt with in this book. But if that is the case, then it has still had its desired effect of causing the player to rethink his original ideas. And it is beyond any shadow of doubt that the ability to question why and to continue to do so keeps the sport alive and well in the eyes of the player. Such inquisitiveness can lead only to the player improving his standards, while there is no telling in what direction squash as a whole can go as a result of perceptive thinking, intense debate, reasoned questioning and more incisive analysis.

The ideas in this book are also for individual interpretation;

Hashim Khan – the 'Grand Old Man of Squash' – signs autographs after the Vintage British Open Final

Susan Devoy of New Zealand wins the British Open final

colour and character should be important facets of the sport, since it would be very dull and restrictive if all players tried to play in exactly the same way. Furthermore, the interesting aspects of other players' games can always form a source of inspiration at worst and lead to new ways of winning matches at best. Variety can also play an integral role in enhancing spectator appeal.

It has not been the intention to spoon-feed the formula for ultimate winning squash. It is assumed that the player is motivated in that direction in any case, so the issues that have been raised can merely create added dimensions and means of reaching the desired end. That goal of winning squash is common to all, but there are so many variations of the way to it that the real craftsman will derive the maximum pleasure from learning the trade – and this applies to all levels. The player can obtain satisfaction from learning to play the sport better, with winning being the end-product, rather than relying on brute force and ignorance allied to physical conditioning.

It is hoped that this philosophy will add to the player's insight into the sport, improve his game in some small way and lead to an enjoyment that makes it all worthwhile.